RAMÓN RODAMILÁNS was born in Bilbao, Spain. He studied music and piano, graduating at Bilbao Conservatoire, and read law at the University of Salamanca. While attending his private business, he wrote several books about Bilbao's Sociedad Filar-mónica and the Spanish composer J C Arriaga. He also wrote *En Irlanda*, his Irish souvenirs.

*Left to right: Austin Coates, the Chinese writer San Liao and RR
Hong Kong, October 1989*

AUSTIN COATES

Souvenirs and Letters

AUSTIN COATES

Souvenirs and Letters

Ramón Rodamiláns

Vale

ATHENA PRESS
LONDON

Austin Coates
Souvenirs and Letters
Copyright © Ramón Rodamiláns 2007

ISBN 10-digit: 1 84748 157 4
ISBN 13-digit: 978 1 84748 157 3

First Published 2007 by
ATHENA PRESS
Queen's House, 2 Holly Road
Twickenham TW1 4EG
United Kingdom

Every effort has been made to trace the copyright holders
of works quoted within this book and obtain permission. The publisher
apologises for any omission and is happy to make necessary changes in
subsequent print runs.

Printed for Athena Press

I: 1987

It was on a hot and humid afternoon, as they usually are in Hong Kong at the end of the rainy season. I believe it was around late September 1987. I went into the big bookshop in Tsim Tsa Tsui, almost at the back of The Peninsula Hotel, and while taking advantage of the cool temperature inside the shop, I enjoyed browsing among the books on China and Hong Kong. I was thus occupied and entertained when, just by chance, a pocket book came into my hands with the appealing title of *Myself a Mandarin*. What actually drew my attention was the name of its author – Austin Coates – and the fact he was the son of the composer Eric Coates, whose musical works – 'London Suite', 'By the Sleepy Lagoon' and many others – I had appreciated since I was a teenager. I took the book with me to my hotel. Once I had started it, I simply could not put it down; it was indeed a fascinating read. What I could never have guessed at that moment was that buying that book would turn out to be the first step in a short but beautiful friendship with its author.

Myself a Mandarin was, and still is, one of the most original and entertaining books I have ever read, a work that is neither history nor fiction. Published by Oxford University Press and Heinemann with the subtitle of 'Memoirs of a Special Magistrate', it recounts some of Austin Coates's experiences in a country district of Hong Kong's New Territories, where he was unexpectedly appointed and served as a special magistrate not long after the Second World War. Sometimes hilarious, sometimes a bit sad, the book was then, and has been ever since, an enjoyable and delightful read, full of understanding and insight into the Chinese – in this case Cantonese – way of thinking. When the book was first published, in 1968, the Cultural Revolution had already been savagely launched, Mao's Red Army was on the border with Hong Kong and, as it has been noted, the frontier was virtually sealed off with all river and train traffic coming to a stop. Ironically, however, as Coates points out, in contrast with earlier Kuomintang interventions, 'Hong Kong [subsequently] settled down to seventeen unprecedented years of tranquillity in its relations with China.'

Shortly after reading *Myself a Mandarin*, and on the advice of a good Hong Kong friend, I found and read *City of Broken Promises*, another Austin Coates book. This one is a historical novel dealing with the period when Portuguese Macao was the sole European outpost in China, and it concerns the moving story of Martha Merop; then came the delightful *A Macao Narrative* and eventually his novel *The Road*. 'Not caring much for the prospect of writing a novel,' he says amusingly in the foreword, 'I decided on a tactic [to discourage his publishers]. I replied: "It's interesting you said that, because I was thinking of writing a novel about a road. It might even in fact be called *The Road*." I calculated that this would put them off sufficiently to make them drop the subject. To my consternation, they said that it sounded very interesting… I was trapped.' It actually was, as he later told me, the story of a woman who is much more intelligent than her husband.

Needless to say, all these books did nothing but whet my appetite for delving deeper into his writings and learning more of his biography. Thus it was my good fortune that two interesting articles on Austin Coates appeared during the following year in two different Hong Kong magazines: the first one in the May issue of *The Peak*, where 'writer Austin Coates reminisces with Jill Entwistle on forty fascinating years in Hong Kong and the Far East'; then, some months later, Barry Parr, in the Cathay Pacific's *Discovery* wrote a very interesting 'Portrait of a Mandarin with Cigar', stating that 'there are few who have captured the colour and the spirit of Hong Kong as well as Austin Coates, a former magistrate turned author who's become as much a part of the Hong Kong landscape as the characters in his books'. But I only very gradually came to learn about the life of Austin Coates himself, a fascinating saga worthy of a full biographical work.

He was the only son of the popular composer Eric Coates and his wife, the talented actress Phyllis Black. As he himself once recalled, 'When you are born, as I was, into music and the arts, it's your life… one took it that one's life would be involved with the arts as a matter of course.'

Austin Coates was born in London, in 1922, and studied at the prestigious public school, Stowe, in Buckinghamshire, and then in Paris, where he contemplated the idea of working in the theatre, both as an actor and playwright. A project for doing a musical comedy with his father – *The Knights of Malta* – was interrupted by the Second World War, which took him with the Royal Air Force, to India, Burma, Singapore and Indonesia up until 1947. Two years later, he very gladly accepted the post of Assistant Colonial Secretary in Hong Kong, and that marked the beginning of his long love affair with the Far East.

Shortly after I had read the above mentioned articles, my friend Diego López, himself an admirer of the writer, took me one day to have lunch at the Bankers' Club, in Hong Kong, and I brought both magazines along with me. He was delighted at reading them, and while we enjoyed our meal and the spectacular sight of the harbour from this elegant restaurant, we talked almost non-stop of Austin Coates and his books. So it was that then and there I decided I had to write Mr Coates a letter. Diego thought it was an excellent idea, and immediately telephoned a friend who knew Coates's exact address in the mid-levels. I made a note of it, and that is how, back in Madrid, I felt bold enough to send my first letter to Austin Coates.

II: 1989

Madrid, 20 February 1989

Dear Mr Coates,

I sincerely apologize for bothering you with this letter, my only excuse being that I have so much enjoyed reading your books I feel I need to thank you for them.

I must confess I bought the first one – *Myself a Mandarin* – out of curiosity, for I'm very fond of your father's nostalgic music. After that, which turned out to be such a pleasant surprise, came *A Macao Narrative*, *City of Broken Promises* and *The Road*, all of which opened up a fascinating new world for me. I therefore wanted to go further into your work, and during my last trip to Hong Kong I called at the Harris Bookshop (in Central) and another good one in Kowloon, looking for *Personal and Oriental*, *Prelude to Hong Kong* and/or some other books of yours, but unfortunately it seems they are rather difficult to find.

Could you possibly tell me where I might look for them? I'd really be most grateful.

Very sincerely yours,

RR

★

It goes without saying that it was an extremely pleasant surprise to receive his very prompt reply a few weeks afterwards, together with a copy of his biography of José Rizal, kindly inscribed. His writing paper was quite original, denoting a very unconventional personality. The letterhead was embossed in bold red letters and simply read:

without any printed address. This was typed below with the rest of the text. (Obviously this meant he could use this stationery all over the world.)

★

Hong Kong, 22 March 1989

Dear Don Ramón,

Thank you so much for your letter of 20 February, and it was a pleasure to learn that you came upon my books by way of my father's music. This is just how life should be.

Personal and Oriental is out of print. I am waiting for the correct moment to ask my publishers to bring it out again. It is a question of timing. (It is about a journey across Asia from Japan to Turkey staying almost entirely in the homes of Asian friends, a journey made in 1952.)

Prelude to Hong Kong has recently been reissued by Oxford University Press, Hong Kong, and would be available on order. It has been renamed *Macao and the British*, its original title when I delivered it as a series of public lectures here in 1952–1953.

However, you have not mentioned the book which I feel that you, as a Spaniard, will find perhaps of special interest, which is my biography of José Rizal, national hero of the Philippines; and I am sending a copy of this, with my very best wishes.

It is a reprint – actually a third edition, just coming to an end – done by Oxford but printed in the Philippines, thus not very well, but it will pass. Another edition will be on its way soon.

Retana – *Vida y Escritos del Dr. José Rizal*, 1907 – wrote the first Rizal biography. Unamuno was so moved when he read Retana's manuscript that he insisted on including an essay of his own, published with it – Unamuno at his best, with all his passionate sincerity.

A succession of unsatisfactory American and Filipino biographies followed. Mine, published by Oxford in 1968, is the direct successor of Retana's. Following in Retana's footsteps, being myself a personal friend and house guest (invariably) of the Rizal family, and bringing to light a good deal more in a gestation period of sixteen years, mine is a more satisfactory biography than Retana's in today's terms. I don't think Retana would begrudge that, either. His admiration of Rizal was the same as mine, and he wished to see the truth told. Anyway, I very much hope you will enjoy it.

It occurs to me that in the summer we live not so far away – within comparatively cheap telephonic range – and thus I enclose my cards. I will be back in Colares on 27 April.

It was a great pleasure to hear from you. It always is, from a discerning reader.

With very best regards,

Austin Coates

------------------∽∞∽------------------

Madrid, 13 April 1989

Dear Mr Coates,

Yesterday, on my return from a business trip, I found your letter and Rizal's biography waiting for me. What a wonderful surprise! It was most kind and generous of you. Thank you very much indeed.

I am ashamed to confess that I know very little about Rizal or, in general, about the Spanish Philippines. In a way it's not so much surprising if you think that when I started school – just after the Spanish Civil War – any criticism against the noble and altruistic achievements of the Spanish Empire was equivalent to *anti-patriotismo*, and history books were written accordingly. I am, therefore, full of excitement at the prospect of delving into your book.

I'm very glad to hear that you are going to spend several months in Portugal. As you said, it's not so far away and I would be delighted to have an opportunity to meet you there.

Since I know a bit about your life – I even read Barry Parr's 'Portrait of a Mandarin with Cigar' – I think it is only fair to let you know something about myself. Unfortunately, there's nothing important.

Born in Bilbao, I studied law and music (piano) and after some hesitation went into the family business – importing and retailing musical instruments, mainly pianos, from Germany, Japan and Korea. Since my first trip to the Far East, seventeen years ago, I have been fascinated by those countries and peoples, and the cultural contrasts between them and the Western world is to me a constant and intriguing subject of reflection. And I must say that I have found your books very illuminating.

I'm writing this to Colares in case it doesn't reach Hong Kong before your departure.

Once again, many thanks for all your kindness.

With my best regards,

RR

--------------------o○o--------------------

Madrid, 28 April 1989

Dear Mr Coates,

I have just finished reading your biography of José Rizal and I think my command of the English language is not good enough to convey to you the very profound impression it has made on me. It would be very difficult to imagine a more convincing portrait of this admirable and fascinating man. I'm not at all surprised that Miguel de Unamuno was so moved when he learnt about Rizal's life.

As a Spaniard, on the other hand, I cannot feel myself very proud of Spain's behaviour in the Philippines. With few, and perhaps remarkable, exceptions, our fellow countrymen are seen in very poor light. As you quite rightly note in your book, the real miracle is that, after all that, the Philippines continued being a Christian country.

I'm glad to tell you that a good friend in Hong Kong has kindly found *Macao and the British* for me, and the book is on its way to Madrid. Needless to say, I'm looking forward to reading and enjoying it, as I always do with your books.

With very best regards,

Yours,

RR

Colares, Portugal, 13 May 1989

Dear Don Ramón

What a great pleasure it was to receive your letter about Rizal, as also to know that you have managed to get *Macao and the British*.

As a Spaniard, although the story of Rizal is hard to take, you need never be in doubt of the contribution which Spain made to Asiatic history. Once arrived in Madrid, Rizal never blamed Spain for the iniquities perpetrated in the Philippines. He blamed the Religious Orders.

Portugal had already flung them out of the country in 1834, as being a scourge and a (blood-sucking) leech. They crept back, and had to be thrown out again in 1911.

Spain in the Philippines represented civilization, as became embarrassingly apparent after 1901, when the Americans took over. The very welcome, modern, but cultureless Americans had nothing to offer to an Asiatic people. Everything of cultural importance in the Philippines, from that day to this, is Spanish.

I am threatening a visit to Madrid, a city I have never been to, in June, coming from Paris. If you are in Madrid around 14–15 June, it would be so good if we could meet. When I get my dates clear, I will endeavour to telephone you.

With very best regards,

Austin Coates

★

And so he did. Almost exactly one month later I received his telephone call – he would never have referred to it as a 'phone call' – but not from Paris. He was already in Madrid.

'Hello, Ramón! It's me, Austin.' Apparently, the geographical nearness had erased formalities and now we were on Christian name terms. He had a very distinct voice and spoke slowly with a beautiful accent. I was both rather surprised and very pleased by his semi-unexpected arrival. He had taken rooms at the Ritz. 'They are very grand,' he said, 'but appallingly expensive!'

I thought to myself that a Ritz Hotel room anywhere in the world was expensive. He was with Yim (Fung Kwai-yim) – his personal assistant – and since evening was coming on, they had planned to have some rest and then eat something light around the hotel before going to bed. I offered several possible programmes for the following day and eventually it was decided to visit Toledo, which with its long history and El Greco background was something very appealing to them. We agreed we would meet next morning at around eleven in the hotel lobby.

It was 14 June, with fine weather and a cloudless sky, although the temperature was already rather high. We were going to have a pretty hot day. So, lightly dressed, I drove to the Plaza de la Libertad, and approaching the hotel saw two persons already awaiting outside, on the kerb. One – according to the photographs I knew – was unmistakably Austin, in an impeccable white shirt worn flowing over his trousers, Filipino-style, and carrying a walking stick. The second one, with a cloth cap and an Asiatic appearance, had to be Yim. Neither of them, however, had any idea of what I looked like or what car I would be driving. So I was quite amazed, when I was still about twenty metres away, to see Yim put up his right arm and point clearly to my car, while saying something to Austin. It was really uncanny. Later on, even Yim was unable to explain to us his intuition. No less extraordinary was how, after correctly greeting each other, we went on our way in the car, chatting easily, like old friends just meeting again after a few weeks of being separated.

Austin, with the perceptive eye of one who has travelled and lived in many countries, was interested in everything we encountered along the route, especially in botanical observation, the irrigation systems and the livestock grazing in the fields; in fact we jumped from one topic to another totally unconnected with the previous one. I wanted, of course, more than anything else to talk about his books. Regarding *City of Broken Promises*, I remember having asked how much of this historical novel was history and how much fiction.

'Well,' he replied, without much hesitation, 'I would say ninety per cent is history. Just by chance, I discovered an oil painting in Macao, in the main room at the Santa Casa de Misericordia. It was the portrait of a woman, and her enigmatic oriental eyes aroused my curiosity. That led me to search the London archives and unravel the story of Martha Merop, the principal character in the book. The rest of the book is my contribution to the story... the artistic side of it,' he added, smiling.

The visit to the old imperial capital was really enjoyable for my new friends. We wandered for a couple of hours about the narrow streets, following almost exactly the obligatory tourist route and stopping at several important places well-known to me. At Santo Tomé, in spite of the crowds, we were able to pause and admire for a while El Greco's masterpiece, *Burial of the Conde de Orgaz*, before visiting his house nearby. It is now – and has been for long time – a charming little museum.

We crossed the road to a sort of garden balcony, impressively hanging over the enormous chasm pierced through the centuries by the River Tajo, which so well justifies its name in this part of Toledo, (*tajo,* meaning cut or cleft in Spanish). On the south bank, in front of us, over the hills, we could imagine the famous *cigarrales* – the so-called Toledo country houses – hidden among the trees. Austin was fascinated looking at the sunken river waters, softly flowing below our feet, and thinking that these same waters, after winding their course for almost 600 kilometres, would meet the sea at Lisbon, under the magnificent suspension bridge (Ponte 25 de Abril) that spans the mouth of the river and which he knew so well. By then, it had changed its name to the Portuguese – *Tejo*.

We went out of the city centre through the Gate del Cambrón, walking downhill (thank God!) the Paseo Recaredo to the Arab Wall and the Hostal del Cardenal, where I had booked a table for lunch. We could already feel the midday heat and were a bit tired after the long walk. The Hostal del Cardenal, an old palace now converted into a pleasant restaurant, was, two centuries ago, the residence of the Cardenal Lorenzana. One goes in through a small but charming garden sheltered by trees. We went up to the first floor dining room and, after ordering some cool drinks, felt relaxed and soon forgot the heat outside. Sensibly, lunch was begun with a very refreshing gazpacho. Then, I was rather surprised to see 'prawns in rice with a hot and spicy curry sauce' included in the menu. In Toledo, of all places! But my amazement was double for, in spite of the heat, both Austin and Yim ordered the prawns without hesitation. The sauce must have been very hot indeed, and it was quite amusing seeing them perspiring, almost in tears, and happily laughing at the same time. Then I realized that both of them, in a way, came from south-east Asia.

Over lunch, I learnt chunks of Yim's adventures in that part of the world. He was a Vietnamese of Chinese origin who fled his country and the communist regime, went to Cambodia, escaped again to Macao and then to Hong Kong. There, in very strange circumstances, he met Austin Coates. Later, I learnt the details of that story. Yim, who had a labouring job at the time, happened to be in Des Voeux Road, in front of the Bank of China. There he saw a European gentleman in the middle of the road, just in the path of two converging trams. Without the slightest hesitation, Yim darted away and pulled him back. 'There's no doubt,' said Austin, when telling me the story, 'at that moment he saved my life.' This took place around 1976.

Yim was very slim then, when we met in 1989, and still is. Shorter than Austin, he spoke several oriental languages besides English and Portuguese, all with a strong Cantonese accent. I gathered that he was then Austin's personal assistant, gardener, cook and private secretary, all rolled into one.

As if we were afraid of going out into the heat again, after lunch (perhaps Austin would had said 'luncheon') we sat out a little longer in the garden while had some coffee. Eventually we went back to the car, and since we had plenty of time, I thought we could make a short detour and have a look at the Royal Palace in Aranjuez. Out on the road, shortly after leaving Toledo, a spectacular thunderstorm broke with heavy rain, and Austin got rather excited looking at the lead-coloured sky. 'Look, the same dark clouds as in El Greco's paintings.'

Once we reached Aranjuez, the storm had temporarily stopped and although it was already too late to pay a proper visit to the interior of the palace, we enjoyed ourselves strolling about the gardens, looking at the beautiful façade and encountering the River Tajo once again. Here it quietly flowed near the palace towards Toledo as in a tree-lined canal, its waters mirroring the overhanging branches on both banks. Late in the evening we were back at the Ritz, three tired but happy people after a pleasant excursion. The rain had brought the temperature down more than 10 ° Celsius.

The following morning they (Austin and Yim) walked to the Museo del Prado – 'literally next door' – and were there for more than two hours. Later, on the telephone, Austin said he had found the Goya collection 'simply overwhelming; above all, the Tapestry Cartoons, when seen all together – uplifting!'

In the evening, Mercedes, my wife, and I had organized a dinner party at home with a small group of English-speaking friends. I was lucky to find a couple of them who had lived in Hong Kong for a time. The heat was again with us, and I told Austin to wear something casual. 'In view of the weather,' he said, 'I thought I would put on a *barong Tagalog*.' This is the elegant creamy Filipino shirt, made of a special fibre produced out of the strong *abaca* leaf of that country, with some embroidery on the front and worn, without a tie, over the trousers.

Austin – very civilized – arrived at the appointed hour, bringing a copy of his father's autobiography, *Suite in Four Movements*, which he presented to me kindly inscribed 'as a souvenir of our first meeting and with esteem and regard'. As the sun was setting behind the buildings, across the little park in front of us, we could feel the evening breeze, still warm but quite pleasant. In Madrid, in the late spring, this is actually the best time of the day. It turned out to be an agreeable party, and Austin enjoyed exchanging opinions with those present who had been to Asia. Yim – an excellent photographer – took some snaps.

The following day, after a second visit to the Prado, they caught the midday express to Lisbon from Chamartin. Although it was a Spanish train, it was named after the Portuguese poet, Luís de Camões.

★

Colares, 6 July 1989

Dear Ramón,

This comes to thank you so much for your wonderful hospitality to us in Madrid, the visit to Toledo, and the lovely evening at your home, with your charming wife and such a delightful group of interesting and attractive friends.

I realized from your first letter to me that you were an exceptional person, but had not, until meeting you, realized quite how exceptional. For me, our meeting was a wonderful experience which I hope will be repeated.

Please forgive this delay in writing. I was under the impression that you would be away in the East for some weeks, and therefore thought I would delay writing till you returned. Then Yim told me that on the contrary you would be in the East only a few days. This so demoralized me that it only added to the delay.

I am hoping very much that we may see you here in September. But before that, Yim is having some enlargements made of the photographs he took, and I will send them when they are ready.

With all good wishes, and with many thanks again,

Very sincerely,

Austin

Madrid, 11 July 1989

Dear Austin,

Back from my trip to Hong Kong and Korea I had to fly again, this time to Germany (Köln) where I spent four days last week, and it is only now that I find the peace of mind to sit down and write this letter.

I have finished reading your father's delightful memoirs, *Suite in Four Movements*. What an interesting and fascinating book! When I listen now to the music of 'London Suite', 'The Three Elizabeths', the 'Saxo-Rhapsody', 'By the Sleepy Lagoon', and so many others, it is a new and wonderful experience, almost like listening to a friend's music. Besides, although I am not a good judge, I have found in your father's writing style a very uncommon charm, maybe the charm of distant days, that made me thoroughly enjoy a very slow reading.

My visit to Hong Kong was, as expected, most interesting and luckily the weather not too bad. I presume you will have read a lot about the latest developments in Peking and HK, Sir Geoffrey Howe's visit to the colony included. I am enclosing herewith a far from soft article by a certain Mr Hicks, whose strong views reflect more or less the prevalent feelings of disappointment towards Britain both among the Chinese and the Western population.

I went into the Hong Kong Book Centre and was fortunate to find another book of yours – *China Races* – and a new Oxford edition of *Myself a Mandarin* with a nice photograph from the old days on the cover. Of course I took both of them with me and I intend to plunge into *China Races* during my fast approaching holidays. We'll be in Monte Carlo until the end of August.

You will also find enclosed some excellent photographs taken by Yim [with my camera]. I hope they will bring you good memories of your short visit to Madrid as they do to me.

With my best regards to Yim,

Yours,

Ramón

Madrid, 20 July 1989

Dear Austin,

Thank you very much indeed for your nice letter, which almost telepathically went its way at the same time as my last one to you. I was so glad to learn you enjoyed your visit to Madrid and Toledo. I do hope it will not be your last trip to Madrid and that we will have further opportunities to pay a visit – perhaps with milder weather – to such interesting places as Segovia, El Escorial etc., all of them a reasonably short drive from Madrid.

Shortly after your departure the strong summer heat arrived here, so we are longing for our holidays in Monte Carlo. Actually we plan to set off next Thursday and will be there for around four weeks. Just in case, my Monaco address is:

7, Avenue St Roman
Monte Carlo

Regarding our possible visit to Portugal in September, I would really be delighted to do it and I do hope that I may escape from Madrid, at least for a few days. If I remember it well, there used to be – in pre-revolution times – a nice small hotel, The Albatroz, in Cascais, looking out over the sea from the top of a cliff. I believe it is still operating, and is not far from Colares. Am I right? Will you be there the whole of September?

I forgot to mention in my last letter that, while I was in Hong Kong, I strolled one morning up and down D'Aguilar Street looking for Rizal's house but I failed to find it. So I turned back to my hotel and took shelter in the coolness of the Captain's Bar, enjoying a perfect dry martini – they really do everything to perfection – and remembering it is also your favourite bar in Hong Kong. However, I could not see the tall barman who, Yim told me, is well acquainted with you.

With all best wishes,

Yours,

Ramón

————○○○————

Monte Carlo, 18 August 1989

Dear Austin,

Once more you have revealed to me a new and fascinating side of Chinese history and Anglo-Chinese relations. Although I'm not very familiar with the world of races, I do love horses and horse riding and have really enjoyed reading *China Races*. What stupendous stories those of 'Bengal', 'Hero', 'Old Bill' and many others! I can fully understand your lines and those quoted from the *North-China Herald* (7 March 1934) at the very beginning of the book. It must have been a tremendous task.

We are approaching the end of our holidays here which have been very healthy, with a lot of swimming, music and reading. I plan to be back in Madrid sometime next week. I will get in touch with you and let you know about our trip to Portugal; I'm looking forward to seeing you very soon.

With all best regards,

Yours,

Ramón

———————o○o———————

Colares, 7 September 1989

Dear Ramón,

Thank you so much for your two letters, and I was fascinated to learn that you had read *China Races*. Actually it was quite fun writing it. Yim, who was my research assistant for the first time on that book, is a racing man. Among other things we did eighty years of the *North-China Herald* and he enjoyed every hour of it. Another great joy was that the *Herald* was one of the best English-language newspapers in the world, and like *The Times* and the *New York Times* it was fully indexed. This saved us an enormous amount of time.

Yim has been through his photographs of our Toledo visit, and doesn't think any of them are good enough to be considered for your magnificent photo album, by which he was tremendously impressed. I have insisted that he must send at least one, so here it is. We must try again in due course.

If you manage a short visit to Portugal this would be splendid, but in any case we will be in touch. I am stuck here at the moment awaiting galley proofs of my latest book. I am here till 17 October, then London, then Hong Kong around 5 November.

It is such a pleasure to me to have come to know you personally. I look forward greatly to our next meeting, wherever it may be.

With great affection,

Austin

★

This meeting was, in fact, shortly afterwards. At the end of September, we eventually managed to make the visit to Colares. After a long drive from Madrid, with a break for lunch at the Parador de Trujillo, we arrived in Cascais late afternoon. Our room at The Albatroz was quite comfortable and decorated in very good taste, and there was a short message from Austin (handwritten) awaiting us:

Dear Ramon,

Will you please telephone me on your arrival.

We would like you to dine with us almost next door to Albatroz - i.e. no more driving. We can be with you from here in forty minutes, including parking.

So good that you are here.

With great affection,

Austin

Presently we met in the hotel bar overlooking the lovely seascape, Estoril on the left and, closer on the right, the little bay of Cascais.

Austin was very happy with a new walking stick I brought him from Madrid for his collection. Quite at home in this country, he ordered *porto branco* as an aperitif. Mercedes had a glass of champagne, and I went for my usual gin and tonic. Yim, as a conscientious driver, did not touch alcohol. We sat down outside, on the veranda, where the evening breeze coming from the sea was cool but pleasant. We were a lively group, glad to be together again after the three summer months.

The restaurant 'almost next door' happened to be a Chinese one, aptly named 'O Dragao'. I remember we enjoyed a rather nice dinner but cannot remember one single word of what we talked about at the table. Probably we were a bit too tired to retain anything in our minds. At a very reasonable hour they left for Colares in Yim's small car and we walked the short distance back to The Albatroz.

The following day, after a good night's sleep, and well break-fasted, I drove along the winding hilly road to Colares. It was narrow but well maintained and we were blessed with a glorious day that made the drive a real pleasure. Austin's small villa was in a quiet and peaceful street – fittingly named Rua das Horas de Paz – hidden among some pine trees. The house, with whitewashed walls and bright red shutters, was surrounded by a garden, also small but luxuriant, full of tropical trees and exotic flowers. José, the smiling Portuguese gardener, was tending a bed of beautiful flowers that were unknown to me. Probably he worked under Yim's instructions. The low wall around the garden was no protection from the curiosity of passers-by or neighbours.

Needless to say we were most warmly welcomed. Yim, all smiles, opened the door and Austin quickly rose to greet us, kissed Mercedes and gave me a big hug. I did not mention before that Austin had white hair (parted on the left side), moved slowly, was a bit shorter than me and of powerful build.

This was more evident now that he wore loose semi-winter clothing. Almost impatiently he asked Yim to bring out the Raposeira, the local sparkling wine, which served cool made a delicious drink. We made ourselves comfortable and only then ventured to look around. The spacious drawing room had a dining area by the windows. In another corner there were a couple of full bookcases and it gave me a certain satisfaction when I recognized several of the titles like Lin Yutang's *The Importance of Living*, Vicky Baum's *Shanghai '37* and *A Tale from Bali*; he had told me once that he was not very fond of reading novels. I also saw some of Han Suyin's autobiographical books and, among the recent publications, Sterling Seagrave's *The Soong Dynasty* and Nien Cheng's *Life and Death in Shanghai*. Later I learnt that they also kept piles of books in their bedrooms upstairs. But after a while, I was somewhat intrigued to notice little holes that went through the pages of some of the old books, holes which could have been made with a piercing device.

'Ah, the red ants!' said Austin. 'When I used to live in Kutching, in Sarawak, they literally ate half of my library. They really were voracious creatures, nothing like the black ones we know here in Europe.'

While we sat down with our drinks, however, the main attraction was a pair of budgerigars, one blue and another green, 'Cinzento' and 'Verde' being their names. Verde was the sociable one and immediately made friends with Mercedes. This amused Austin, who said to me, 'Look, Mercedes is coming to terms with Verde.' Yim, quick with his camera, took a shot of this 'friendship'.

As a matter of fact, Yim's camera has been of great help to me now in going back over our steps during that first day in Colares. For, after we left, he sent me a few photographs to Madrid with some texts written by Austin in the back, so I can now not only retrace our movements of that day but I can very clearly see us across the distance of fifteen years.

When we were through with the Raposeira, we drove to lunch at Casa da Ponte, a nice, unpretentious restaurant in Praia das Maças. It was quite late by local standards, and all the tables were empty. I cannot forget Austin's exclamation on seeing them, 'Oh look! The choice is overwhelming.'

When we were sitting at the table, Yim took one of his shots at the very moment Austin was earnestly pointing his index finger at me, while Mercedes and I attentively listened to his explanation. Jokingly, he wrote later, 'You can imagine what it was like when I was a Magistrate.'

Azenhas do Mar was – and I suppose still is – another charming coastal village where we took a pleasant walk in the afternoon. It is up on a cliff, with splendid views of the Atlantic and a long stretch of coastline to Ericeira in the far distance. The seafront of these villages was filled with low houses perched on the cliffs, all white with red tiles, of new construction, that looked to me like holiday homes. In these parts, although the terrain slopes sharply, the sand beaches are almost flat and the long waves arrive gently after breaking far away from the shore. One of the most beautiful of these beaches, north of Azenhas, is Praia da Aguda, which we also visited some time later that afternoon. The view from the top of the *largo* – the promenade and containing wall over the beach – was breathtaking. On the wall, written on colourful painted tiles we could read this:

> LARGO
> DA PRAJA
> DA AGUDA
> Gosto de ti, tanto, tanto!
> Este gosto nunca muda,
> És um verdadero encanto
> Oh linda Praia de Aguda!

On our way to Colares we stopped at the most unusual round hermitage of Sao Mamede, outside a place called Janas, near Sintra. It looked like a mini-bullfighting ring; the centre was covered with red tiles, and round the tiles there was built something like the roof of a hut made with branches. Inside it was totally empty. It seemed to be very old. Not even Austin knew when it dated from, but for some reason he was very intrigued by it.

In the evening, back at the Rua das Horas de Paz, we very peacefully sat again to rest and consume another refreshing bottle of Raposeira before driving back to Cascais. As a farewell present, Austin had a nice surprise for me. It was a double LP record album of his father's music – *The Music of Eric Coates* – conducted by the composer himself and covering his compositions from

1910–1937. It had been released three years before by The Vintage Light Music Society, in celebration of Coates's birthday centenary. On the album cover there was a well-known photograph of the composer, holding his inevitable cigarette. Austin told us then the little story of his father and his 'inevitable cigarette'. Eric Coates, a heavy smoker, always smoked Turkish cigarettes. On one occasion the doctor told him to stop smoking – he suffered from asthma – and so he did for three years, during which he could not compose a single original work. Until one day, fed up with this situation, he said to himself, To hell with doctors! and started smoking again. 'And you know what happened?' said Austin. 'In a few days he wrote "The Dambusters"!' Anyway, I was very happy indeed with my album.

Mercedes and I went the following day to Lisbon to have lunch with a charming young lady, a good friend of ours, and in the evening we were again the guests at a dinner party organized by Austin. This time it was in Cascais, with his English cousins Gerald and Graciette Gibbon, who happened to live there, and some friends of Austin's from Macao, Gilbert and Justina Wells, who had a house in Azenhas do Mar. There were some other people whose names I cannot remember, not even their faces. The dinner was al fresco, in the little garden of the restaurant O Puccaro. There was, however, something in particular about that evening that I distinctly remember. I was sitting next to Graciette and near Yim, and was – in some way – surprised by their apparent intimacy, joking and teasing each other. I say this because, after Austin's death, I learnt that this friendship suddenly stopped. Anyway, the party was very lively and went on well into the small hours. I also recall having thought how amusing life can be at times: there we were, sitting in completely unfamiliar surroundings, chatting easily to eight or ten people who, only three months before, we had not known at all.

We didn't want to go back to Madrid without visiting Sintra, especially the admirable and incongruous Palacio da Pena, so we did this by ourselves for most of the next day. In the evening, we enjoyed our last dinner with Austin and Yim. This time they were our guests at Porto Santa Maria, a good fish and seafood restaurant on the beaches of Gincho. We were offered special crabs as a delicacy, and this was the excuse that led Austin to talk of the Macao crabs. 'Probably the best in the world,' he said, 'whatever they say in China of the Shanghai crabs.' But he explained the great difference in both cases and the crabs in Europe. 'It is the way of killing them. Here, in Europe, they are hurled alive into boiling water, thus dying in agonising pain, their sinews tense, making the meat almost uneatable. The Chinese way is to introduce a chopstick through its mouth, pressing gently until you realize the crab is dead. It has died without any pain. Then the meat is the most delicious you can taste, only obtainable in that part of the world.'

Austin completed his 'lecture' on crabs, advising us 'never to buy them at a new moon or full moon, for at these times crabs rush about on the floor of the sea, the males pursuing the females, the females pretending desperately to run away; and as result of all this activity, all end up very thin'. Needless to say, after this detailed information we put crabs out of our minds, and ordered different sorts of prawns that looked very appetizing. We were eating literally by the seashore, which added to the pleasure of such a good meal. In a way, our trip to Portugal resembled a gastronomic marathon, but we could hardly help it.

It was a marvellous starry evening, and back in The Albatroz I opened the doors on the balcony to gaze at the stars for a moment. Then we felt, like a pleasant tonic, the smell of the sea brought in by the night wind.

★

Madrid, 3 October 1989

Dear Austin,

As planned, we drove back to Madrid, rather sorry to leave. It was so good to see you again and spend such a pleasant time together. Mercedes joins me in thanking you most sincerely for your warm hospitality. We keep a really delightful memory of this short visit to Cascais and Colares.

This makes me realize I left without taking the address of your charming cousins, Gerald and Graciette. Will you please give them our best regards and tell them how grateful we were for that enjoyable evening and dinner at O Puccaro? I hope the Spanish-Portuguese postal services do not fail me, and that this letter arrives before your departure to London.

The two-record album with your father's recordings is simply wonderful, with some music I had never heard before, like the 'Symphonic Rhapsody' (including my favourite song 'Birdsongs at Eventide'). It is really surprising how well the recordings are made and preserved, considering some of them are over fifty years old. Needless to say, listening to his voice – even in that short speech – is very moving. Many thanks once again.

Over the weekend we went for lunch with some musician friends to a restaurant in the old part of Madrid, and just by chance I found out they are also the managers of El Hostal del Cardenal, where we lunched together in Toledo. I took the enclosed card, thinking you might like to keep it.

I am trying to delay my trip to Hong Kong for a few days so that I am still there when you arrive. My good friend Diego López Alonso, who lives in Hong Kong (he is the manager of a Spanish bank there) has read many of your books and would be more than happy to meet you personally. Maybe with a bit of luck we might enjoy a dinner together.

I will telephone you when I have my dates clear.

My best regards to Yim.

Yours ever,

Ramón

Colares, 10 October 1989

Dear Ramón,

Many thanks for your letter of the 3rd, and for the Hostal del Cardenal card, which I was delighted to have. I had thought to ask for one when we were there, and then forgot.

My cousin is Sra D [sic] Graciete Gibbon, Companhia Portu-
guesa de Resseguros, Rua Alexandre Herculano 27, Lisboa 12.
(The 12 has been changed to thousands, but no one ever uses the
postal numbers anyway – like seat belts in Spain.)

Actually I had already conveyed your message verbally to her
and Gerald; they say they hope you and Mercedes will come
again. They are at present in Florence attending a conference – on
insurance, if you please. (The insurance value of the David?)

Yim and I are booked to return to Hong Kong on 27 October.
I very much hope we shall be able to meet there, and would very
much like to meet and entertain Diego López Alonso. Let us hope
things work out this way.

I am absolutely delighted with my walking stick. Thank you
very much.

Love to you both,

Austin

PS I was fascinated to hear that you had put on the historical Eric
Coates records. One can hardly believe it, but the 'Joyous Youth'
valse, recorded in 1923, was a mechanical sensation. Excitement
in the trade was tremendous. It was the first time the bass notes
came over properly without breaking the wax. I suspect that my
father himself had something to do with this. He was extremely
careful about 'balancing', long before professional 'balancers'
existed.

Later, around 1930, the recording companies got so carried
away by being able to reproduce the bass that they frequently
produced distortions.

★

On 24 October, I flew to Hong Kong via Bangkok with Thai
Airways, and upon arrival I went straight away to The Mandarin
and to the Captain's Bar for lunch. In the evening, I met Diego at
the Harlequin on the twenty-fifth floor, with the very impressive
view of the harbour and the Kowloon peninsula glittering with
thousands of lights that rose and faded into the northern hills. I
could never get tired of Hong Kong and its particular charm. It is

true that one cannot speak highly of large places, like Lon~~~
New York for instance, without reserve. And this of course a~
applies to Hong Kong. There are always two sides to a coin. In a
colonial world we will always find a Kipling and an Orwell. But it
is also true that some cities, some places, no matter how comfortable or uncomfortable, how exciting or dull, have a special appeal
for certain people. It is that something – as Cole Porter would
have put it – which gets under one's skin. I must confess that
since the first time I saw Hong Kong, many years ago, I got it
under my skin. It is not easy to explain, but no explanation is
necessary.

I believe I was more or less thus reflecting one evening while I
was having dinner with Diego and Mimi, his lovely Chinese wife
from Macao. We were at L'Opera, then a fashionable restaurant in
Lan Kwai Fong, the bustling area of ceaseless human traffic in
Central, where expatriates and also Chinese crowded in numberless bars and restaurants until early morning. Many of these
enjoyed only ephemeral success, if any at all. Probably, L'Opera
has long since disappeared. Nevertheless, this could be seen as an
example of the entrepreneurship and resilience of Hong Kong
people.

Austin arrived early in the morning two days later, and as if
thinking nothing of a twelve-hour non-stop flight from London,
he went first thing to the barber's shop to have his hair cut and
then to his dear Foreign Correspondents' Club in Lower Albert
Road, made famous by Richard Hughes and others of his type.
Austin also rang up at The Mandarin and asked me to join him
and San Liao for lunch. 'She is a very charming lady from
Singapore whom you will like to meet,' he explained.

She actually was a Chinese writer based in Singapore and a
good friend of Austin's. She had planned to visit Peking for a few
days before returning to the island state. The meeting place was
Jimmy's Kitchen, a well-known Anglo-Chinese restaurant, also in
Central, with a long tradition by Hong Kong standards. There
were four of us: Austin, San Liao, Yim and myself.

Although more than four months had elapsed since the
Tiananmen 'incident' – the euphemism which would have been
used between the wars – the Peking massacre was an unavoidable

ion those days, especially in Hong Kong, where
ıt 1997 was looming large. It was San Liao's
ıg to find out the true feelings of Chinese people
oint, one of the others mentioned the shameful
ıao Tse-Tung (two volumes) written by the
:morialist Han Suyin, and since I could not
swallow her cynical approach to recent Chinese history, and her
lies and 'contradictions' regarding the Cultural Revolution, I
candidly said so. I also reminded my friends of that episode in *My
House has Two Doors*, where she tells the 'sad' story of Nien Cheng
committing suicide in Shanghai because she could not endure her
daughter's condemnation of her. The very *sad* reality was that her
daughter, Meiping, far from accusing her mother, was assassinated during the Cultural Revolution, and Nien Cheng, far from
taking her own life, left China, wrote *Life and Death in Shanghai* in
1986, and was living in Washington DC. 'She was,' wrote Nien
Cheng of Han Suyin in her book, 'my former Yenching school-
mate.' None of my table companions had compared the texts of
the two books.

At one time, Han Suyin lived in a villa in Singapore with
servants and gardeners, while 'deeply' sharing in her heart the
miserable suffering of her people in China. It was, as Simon Leys
wrote with irony, 'the Double Vision of Han Suyin.' As I knew
she had been an old acquaintance of Austin's when he lived in
Kuala Lumpur, and feeling that I had perhaps said too much, I
tried to soften the tone, in a way to apologize for been so out-
spoken; but he cut in quickly, 'No, no, Ramón, you're perfectly
right. Communist history will bear little relation to what actually
happened, and, of course, she followed "her masters".'

This led Austin and San Liao to reminisce about the old days
in Singapore and their mutual friends there, while Yim and I
talked of our recent trip to Portugal. Before saying goodbye, San
Liao promised to bring down the latest news from Peking, which
I would receive through Austin.

That evening, I was supposed to go up to Austin's place in
Macdonnell Road, and Yim very kindly came to fetch me at The
Mandarin to avoid my getting lost within the maze of Hong Kong
mid-levels. We found Austin reading the biography of Napoleon

III and Eugénie, written by Jasper Ridley. He found it very interesting and said it might also be of interest to Mercedes, so I made a note of the book. He closed it, of course, politely and came to sit with us. While Yim went for glasses and a chilled bottle of champagne, he took out a Javan cigar.

'Would you mind if I smoke a cigar?' he asked. 'I don't smoke many during the day, but I like one or two in the evening with my drinks.' I didn't mind, of course. At that time I also used to smoke cigarettes. Besides, we were sitting with the windows open. 'You see,' he said, 'I'm probably the only person without air conditioning in this part of Hong Kong. Since I also work at home, as you know, I cannot write in the claustrophobic atmosphere of a tightly closed room. I need the windows open, to listen to the birds and feel the fresh air. Well, it's more natural.' Then he recalled, 'When I first came to Hong Kong in 1949, you could count on the fingers of one hand the number of buildings that were fully air-conditioned. It was very rare indeed.'

I thought that air conditioning started – like so many things – in the United States and said so.

'Oh, no!' exclaimed Austin, amused. 'It all started in Calcutta, in the early twenties.' And going back to 1949, he recalled the Gloucester Hotel facing the old post office in Des Voeux Road. He paused, searching his memory. 'Yes, it was a fine hotel, an eight- or ten-storey building. One day they decided to install air conditioning in just ten bedrooms. They cost a little bit more and were never occupied, except on the few occasions when some Americans were visiting the city.' And he added, half smiling, 'Let's face it, Ramón, in those years, having air conditioning in one's bedroom was considered a *bit wet*.'

The muffled noise of night traffic down in Central came through the windows, which opened on to a balcony. Looking around, I immediately remembered what Jill Entwistle wrote in her article for *The Peak*. Austin lived in 'unexpected modest surroundings among an assortment of furniture whose only common ground appears to be its disregard for interior designers'. He was very proud, however, of his important collection of paintings by the Indian artist Jamini Roy, which one could see hanging on almost every wall. The artist himself, a personal friend, thought of this collection as the most representative body of his work, and Austin told me he was considering leaving it to some Portuguese institution. The paintings were not exactly to my liking – too far away, perhaps, from my elementary knowledge of painting styles – but they blended quite well within that half-exotic, half-Chinese atmosphere.

'I'm thinking of taking you to a rather unusual Chinese restaurant,' Austin announced when it was time to go out for dinner. 'At least, I believe it will be unusual for you. We shall take our own wine with us,' he added, laughing softly.

And it was indeed unusual. We went down to the old Chinese district in Queen's Road West, which was, Austin explained, the original seashore line when Victoria was founded before all the subsequent land reclamations. This was really amazing, almost incredible; but, of course, if you think about it, it was not in the least surprising. The steep Victoria peak goes into the sea with the same inclination it has outside the water, so all flat land in this area must have been reclaimed from the sea.

A mixture of pleasant and unpleasant smells pervaded those dark streets of old Hong Kong, which seemed to be wrapped in mystery; one had the sensation of walking into an old black and white movie about the Chinese underworld. We found the Tau Kee restaurant in a basement, after going through a jumble of stairs. It had no decoration, just the bare essentials. Austin told me that before being upgraded into a restaurant, it was simply an alley *dai pan dong* without even a roof. The owner, a rather old man, all sinews, wore only a white singlet (perhaps now not so white) over his shorts, and Yim called him 'Uncle', the familiar but respectful Chinese way of addressing an elder. He and his family – we could probably see three generations there – were Chiu Chow (or Teochew) people from the most easterly and poorest parts of Guangdong province and Uncle, as many others, retained their own dialect. Austin let me know, *en passant*, that the most prominent member of the Chiu Chow community – or any community in Hong Kong, for that matter – was the billionaire Li Ka-Shing.

We had brought down two bottles of chilled white wine, which was not quite so chilled by the time we had reached the restaurant. So Austin immediately asked for an ice bucket. One of Uncle's sons brought it and, without blinking, helped himself to a nice glass of our wine. Yim looked at me and said, smiling, 'That's why I brought down two bottles.' The Chiu Chow food was not exactly to my taste. Eatable, yes, but not particularly tempting. Obviously, this view was not shared at all by my two friends, and this soon became clear to me. All in all however, we had a very pleasant time, and I was quite glad to have known this 'unusual' place, as Austin called it, which was indeed a far cry from the tourist beaten track.

On my last day in Hong Kong, we eventually met up with Diego. Before lunch we gathered for drinks at the Captain's Bar, so dear to Austin and me. Diego had brought some of Austin's books to have them inscribed. After drinks, we walked to the Furama Inter-Continental nearby, where Austin had booked a table at the top floor restaurant for the most luscious buffet lunch I had ever seen. Yim, who already knew about it, had been looking forward to it since the day before. There was Western, Japanese and, of course, Chinese food, all of it excellent. This place had another important and attractive feature: it was a revolving restaurant, and the splendid views of the city, the harbour and the Kowloon peninsula passed before us like in a slow motion film. It was quite entertaining. From time to time, Austin drew our attention to some point of special interest. (It is a pity that this prestigious building, like the Hilton Hotel, and many others in Central, have now been pulled down, to make room for a more profitable and higher office space.) The meeting with Diego was, from a different point of view, a great success. He had lived for a long time in Manila, spoke Tagalog, and obviously knew Rizal's story very well. All this came as a wonderful surprise to Austin, who was fascinated in exchanging views with him about life in the Philippines.

Down in Connaught Road, after this most pleasant lunch, we bade adieu to each other. I went to the airport and quietly left for Bangkok.

★

Hong Kong, 12 November 1989

Dear Ramón,

It was such a pleasure seeing you here, and I only wish I could have organized things better socially; but our first weekend back here is always rather a muddle.

What I wanted to say was that that biography of Napoleon III and Eugénie, which we thought Mercedes might be interested in, is very heavy going. It announces at the beginning that it is a personal biography, but in fact it is a very complicated blow-by-blow political account, which in places I found very trying, and which I think may prove to be too much even for Mercedes!

One good thing about it: the author goes into many of the poisonous and nasty things related of Eugénie, and demolishes nearly all of them – for those with patience.

What you said here about repudiated commercial contracts with China was last week virtually spelled out in an official announcement from Peking. It actually referred to foreign-owned land and property in China, on which a freeze has been placed. But of course it means more than this.

It looks to me as if West German interest in East Germany, the question of Austria, plus Mrs Thatcher, will combine to produce a milk-and-water EEC. But perhaps this is wishful thinking.

I find the twilight atmosphere of Hong Kong rather depressing. In fact, both Yim and I are already looking forward to being back in Europe. We do not usually reach this stage till around February.

With very best wishes to you both, and our hope of seeing you next year in Madrid,

Very affectionately,

Austin

Madrid, 13 November 1989

Dear Austin,

I hope that you may like to keep these photographs I am enclosing as a souvenir of our very pleasant meetings in Hong Kong. It was indeed, for me, a wonderful time that we spent together and I enjoyed every minute of it. This also comes to thank you most sincerely for your very kind hospitality, the long evenings – always too short – chatting of almost everything under the sun and drinking lots of champagne...

I am sending two copies of the photograph taken by Yim in front of Jimmy's Kitchen so that you can pass one on to your very good friend, Mrs San Liao. She struck me as a charming and very clever woman. Could you, by the way, recommend some of her writings to me?

Unfortunately I am back to my busy life in the office and struggling to find some spare time for my reading and my piano. Sometimes this is not so easy.

Now I am about to go through *Commerce in Rubber*, which looks very promising, and I have been lucky to find, through Hatchards in London, another book of yours, *China Consuls* which also sounds most interesting. It will, I hope, arrive soon.

All my best regards to Yim.

Yours ever,

Ramón

--------------------∽◯◦--------------------

Monte Carlo, 7 December 1989

Dear Austin,

Thank you very much indeed for your letter and warning against Napoleon and Eugénie's biography. Unfortunately this last came too late, for by then I had already ordered the book from Hatchards. However it doesn't matter much, for after all, as you said, there is always some positive point in this, as in most well-researched books.

Following your advice I brought with me to Monte Carlo and have started reading Vicki Baum's *Shanghai '37*, which has been sitting for so long in my library. It is a fascinating book, and I am absolutely amazed by her deep knowledge of so many different cultures and historical backgrounds. Or so it seems to me. She is a very fine storyteller and her characters are so true to life they seem to walk out from between the pages.

The other day I was listening to a small orchestral work by Frank Bridge – 'Cherry Ripe' – and to my great surprise there I found the central theme of your father's 'Covent Garden'. I was puzzled until I discovered that both Eric Coates and Frank Bridge used the same well-known traditional tune for their pieces.

Talking of music, I want to tell you about a marvellous discovery I have recently made: the first violin concerto by Béla Bartók. It is the more surprising since Bartók is by no means one of my favourite composers, but this concerto by the younger Bartók – maybe his mind was not yet corrupted – has to my taste a very strong appeal and lyrical content. There is a beautiful recording made by the no less beautiful Korean violinist, Kyung Wha Chung, with the Chicago SO under Solti. Are you already familiar with this work?

The news coming out from China is, as you said, very disturbing although looking at the rapid changes taking place in Eastern Europe, who can dare to prophesy anything for China and Hong Kong as far ahead as 1997? But perhaps this too is wishful thinking.

Since this letter will reach you near Christmas days I want to send to you and Yim all my very best wishes for a merry Christmas and a happy New Year. Or shall I say *Kung Hey Fat Choy*? Mercedes too wishes you both all the best, and we sincerely look forward to seeing you next spring in Madrid.

Yours ever,

Ramón

Hong Kong, 18 December 1989

Dear Ramón,

Thank you so much for sending the photographs taken during your Hong Kong visit, and for sending the extra one for San. She was delighted, and asks me to thank you. She leaves at the end of the month to resume residence in her native Singapore, and went up to Peking last weekend to see how things were. She says it's very depressing. Even the small tea houses, half empty these days, seem very quiet, people just sitting there smoking, hardly any talk. The military are everywhere; they've put them in police uniforms – to deceive whom? The T'ien An Mên, where the massacre took place in June, is totally forbidden ground. No one is allowed to enter it – for fear some of them sit down (this is literally true).

But of course a bit of the Peking humour remains. A drinking toast between trustworthy friends is: 'Nobody was killed.'

The American magazine *Asiaweek* (*Newsweek*'s cousin) has just started a press campaign to say that there was not massacre – the Americans are that desperate for business in China, one assumes. One of San's closest friends in Peking was actually in T'ien An Mên square on 4 June, and saw the tanks rolling over and crushing living human beings, most of them lying down or sitting.

Yim and I were going over to the Philippines for Rizal Day (30 December), but at the first alert on radio that another coup had been attempted, Yim insisted that we cancel the visit. As a Knight Commander of the Order of Rizal, I have to do the Rizal death march, from Fort Santiago to the Luneta, and, led by the Chief Justice and with so many prominent men from all over the country, we are terribly exposed. This has always been the charm of it. Until we actually reach the Luneta the crowd hold themselves back, with a policeman here and there, just for decoration.

But in this situation, when no one is in control of the armed forces, anything could happen; and Yim, an escapee from first Vietnam, then Cambodia, reads the signals correctly. Also, the Rizal family, with whom I always stay, live totally defenceless, in what was, when I first knew it, a grassy country area, but is now impacted with thousands of shanty huts. Foreign guests merely attract attention to them.

It sounds ridiculous to take such precautions, but one must be sensible and not walk into silly situations. I have walked into numerous dangerous situations, in which I myself was the focal point. But they were not silly situations. I never walked into any of them until I was fairly sure that I'd lined things up so as to be able to carry it off, without being assassinated or badly damaged.

I have rather a special approach to military or civil disorder in other people's countries.

So has Yim!

So there we are. We cut Filipinas and go to Singapore direct, because I want to go to Malacca to see what the Malaysia government is doing when it says it is 'restoring' the Portuguese remains. I'm also interested in knowing what's going on about picking up the 'loot' of Albuquerque in that ship, *Flor do Mar*, or something like that, which sank in the Strait of Malacca.

One will never learn anything about this from the people concerned. I know Malacca so well, so long (since 1946), and have so many contacts that I don't think it will be necessary to ask directly.

You have to have a sieve, of course.

Your letter from Monte Carlo has this moment arrived. I am fascinated by what you say about the Bartók violin concerto, and will obtain a recording here – I share your views on Bartók. Something went mysteriously wrong with all those gifted composers of that time. They addled; the egg was neither productive nor edible. One day I must tell you what I had related to me of that strange period – probably 1923–1925 – when something seemed to die in the composers' musical imagination. It was as if they were daunted by the light, sought refuge in darkness, and then a portcullis (of intellectualism) descended, shutting them off for ever.

As a result, the mainstream of world music simply moved to Jerome Kern, George Gershwin, and to Romberg and Oscar Strauss, to say nothing of Franz Léhar, who was in any case already established. Concert halls became mausoleums, and have remained so: temples for the propitiation of the dead, usually symbolized by a bust of Beethoven as you brave the door of the devotees.

It is no use my telling you. You know more about music than I ever will, and your competence as a pianist is so lovely that one is left speechless. With you, I am in the presence of great musicianship, as your friend Rubinstein left testimony.

Yim sends some photographs. My favourite is the one of Mercedes trying to get the bird to pay attention.

We will all be in touch when the spring comes, if not before.

With great affection,

Austin

III: 1990

Madrid, 5 February 1990

Dear Austin,

Thank you very much indeed for your letter of 18 December and Yim's extremely fine photographs. I think I will have to appoint him my official photographer. Mercedes is especially happy with his excellent portrait of my humble self. All of them bring back to mind our very pleasant visit to Colares.

Your news about the situation in Peking – despite Peking humour – is really depressing, and the campaign started by *Asiaweek*, simply disgusting. There should be a limit to businessmen's greediness. Or perhaps one is asking for too much.

Speaking of music, what you say about post-1920 composers is absolutely true. I would add that a kind of musical snobbery – Thackeray could not even think of it – invaded the 'serious' music field at that time and has stayed with us since then. Critics did not dare to speak their minds – lest they were considered not clever enough – thus spreading that intellectual disease and conditioning the less independent minds of the generally uncultivated audiences. This unfortunate mental attitude has been – in my opinion – responsible for Tchaikovsky or Rachmaninov being often rated second-class composers, while Stockhausen or John Cage were being promoted to eminence. Years ago I used to read the *New Yorker* magazine, because Winthrop Sergeant, then the writer in charge of 'musical events', was the only critic I knew who dared to call a spade a spade. I confess I enjoyed seeing Anton Webern and the likes being dragged to the scaffold.

A few weeks ago I found a Spanish translation of your book on numerology and I must say, after having read it, I am absolutely fascinated by this world of numbers. I knew nothing about it before and, obviously, I will need more than one reading to become somehow familiar with this science.

I have, however, attempted to draw my own *rejilla* (I don't know the correct English word) and although I do not feel able to 'read' it, I have got the impression that it looks interesting. I realize, of course that my name being a long one, the number of rings has less value. But all the same, there are several rings apparently in good numbers. Could I possibly ask you for help? I would very much appreciate having your opinion on my numbers. My date of birth is 11 June 1932. If I did a correct calculation, I am 5 by name and also 5 by birth, the *equilibrador* being 1. Is that so?

I have very much enjoyed Chapters 16 and 17 as I am too a great admirer of both Noël Coward – in all his multi-talented ways – and Bette Davis. It is curious you precisely mention the film *Now Voyager*, for to me it is one of her best movies and certainly one of my favourites. Perhaps Max Steiner's delightful music and Walt Whitman's mini-poem are partly responsible for my being so fond of it.

You were probably very surprised when I said in one of my letters that I was waiting for your book *China Consuls* to come from Hatchards. As you see from the enclosed copy, it was not my fault or mistake but Whitaker's bookbank's. I was much puzzled when I received the book and saw it was written by a certain P. D. Coates. By the way, did you know anything about him? Of course, I wrote back to Hatchards and they have already replied saying that their bookbank has been amended accordingly.

Today I will probably finish reading *Commerce in Rubber*, which I am finding most interesting indeed. It is amazing to see how the history of rubber develops and become interwoven little by little with the history of man. I think I never told you that some years ago I was much involved in that dangerous game: the commodity exchange. Therefore I have relived – reading your book – my thrilling days of Mincing Lane and Plantation House. I dealt in several commodities, but – I don't know why – never with rubber. Probably, as you say, Singapore was already the very centre of the rubber trade, and I was too far away, even mentally.

Now, on the contrary, the spring is not too far away and you will be already making plans to come over to Europe. Please let me know if you wish to pay a visit to Madrid. We would be delighted.

Yours ever,

Ramón

Colares, 23 June 1990

Dear Ramón,

Prior to getting down, at last, to write a letter in reply to yours of last February (!), I have done your numbers. Yes, they are very good, and very strong. And you have of course done them correctly, two 5s with 1 as the *equilibrador*. On the *rejilla* – the word I use is 'grid' – I was surprised that music is not stronger; it is there, of course, on 3, sending out strong signs in a successful commercial direction – larger 6, and even stronger 9. If your father had asked me to do these numbers, this would have foxed me, unless he had told me the nature of his own business, when I might have guessed it. But this is tricky. Basically, this is the *rejilla* of a very literary and successful businessman and organizer. I would have said that you would be musical, but would have probably left it at that.

I put it like this, because doing children's numbers is where numerology is most useful. One can often warn parents about things to watch out for as their children grow up.

My father first introduced me to the subject, when I was eleven (1933). During the winter school term he'd seen an article on it in the *Evening News*, and cut it out for me – why, I cannot imagine. When I got home to London for the winter holiday he gave me the cutting, saying, 'I thought this might interest you.' And for some incomprehensible reason it did. I soon discovered that most of the article was nonsense. At Christmas I did the numbers of two of my aunts, in their presence, and we all laughed until we cried. But during the war, in the bombings, and particularly on the Air Force, surrounded by dozens of people, all young and all worried about the future, I did hundreds of people's numbers, and found out by experience what the numbers really mean. Then, at the end of the war, in Rangoon in 1945, I suddenly realized the *rejilla*, and how it works.

Some of the letters I received, many years later, from men whose numbers I'd done in writing, with predictions, are extraordinary, quite uncanny, showing without doubt that there must be something in it. In each case the writer had totally forgotten about my predictions, long before (in one case) even the first one came true. Years later my written predictions had come to light. In one instance, a wife clearing out a long disused cupboard – and there it all was. I think it may have been partly this that made me write the book, in 1973.

One of the funny ones did not come in the form of a letter. My commanding officer in Bengal, a highly-decorated pilot, aged twenty-seven, was dying to get back to what he called 'Civvy Street'. He went on and on about it until I, for one, was bored to death with him. One day he asked me to do his numbers. Alas! Having done them, I was obliged to tell him that four years from now he would still be in uniform. It was 1945. I told him I did not expect the Japanese war to last more than another two years; but there it was: four years from now he would still be in uniform.

He was so angry that he literally never spoke to me again. Happily, a week or two later, I went forward into Burma, and saw the last of him.

Four years later, early in 1949, I was in London, where I received a telephone call from a former Air Force colleague. Did I remember our commanding officer in Bengal? (Indeed I did; insupportable young man.) He had asked that a message be delivered to me; he thought it might interest me. He was Air Attaché to the British Ambassador in Washington.

(At that time, still in the aftermath of war, he would probably have been wearing uniform every day.)

And he did have the courtesy to go to great pains to send me the message – without committing himself in writing, of course. 'Diplomats' have to be careful.

I have so healthy a respect for numerology that I seldom do people's numbers, and never in front of them. Sometimes, looking at the *rejilla*, and checking against the three main numbers, you see some utter obstacle opposing itself to their hopes and ambitions. It is very easy for intelligent people to read from my face what is going on in my mind. The sudden shock which I experience on meeting with adverse numbers in someone else will be conveyed to that person. Thus, never in front of anybody.

Even with parents bringing to me an infant's numbers, or a growing child's, having asked the various questions in order to determine what precise name the child is likely to be called by (this often takes quite a time), I asked them to go home and come back next day or when it suits them.

I have an horrifying lesson of the importance of this. It was when I was actually writing the numerology book.

We were in Penang, in my former house – a small palace standing secretly in at least twelve acres of tropical fruit trees and garden, one of the most fascinating dwellings in the Orient. When, in 1960, I had rented it, having found it – I was First Secretary in the British High Commission and was expected to live in a hotel – my landlord was Willie, young, incisive, hilarious, and probably a millionaire; Chinese, of course.

Willie was so amazed by what I did with this old and almost abandoned house – a few weeks after I moved in, it was described in the national press as the most beautiful house in Malaya – that, when I left, in 1962, Willie himself took it over.

On my return to Penang – in connexion with writing *Islands of the South* – in 1971, Willie said, why on earth did I not take over the servants' quarters. So I did. They were about three times the size of your apartment in Madrid, and of course Willie and I shared this magnificent place and garden.

Willie had a son, aged about seven, with an ungovernable temper. He was a really horrid little boy, cruel even to his own mother, and a child who would never be able to make friends. One evening Willie, who breezed in and out of the servants' quarters whenever he felt so inclined, asked me to do the boy's numbers. I put a sheet of paper on the closed lid of the piano, and was making up the *rejilla*, when Willie was called to answer the telephone in the 'palace'. Thank heaven he was, because a moment later I put the lines on the *rejilla*, and there was the Greek cross.

Even there, so close to the equator, I went cold all over. I knew what the Greek cross meant, but I had never done one. It means 'speechless', or ungovernable temper, or insanity, and points to self-destruction. I hastily tore the paper into very small pieces, and threw it away; and when Willie came back I diverted his attention to other matters. But I had a real shock, because that *rejilla* was that boy – just so.

I often wonder what became of that child. Willie's wife, a charming woman, bore him another son soon after, and then they all moved to Vancouver. I met Willie some years later – we both happened to visit Penang at the same time – and it was perhaps significant that he never mentioned his elder son.

One of the best numerologists was the New York dance band leader Lopez – was he Frank Lopez? I can't remember – who used to do people's numbers from the dance floor, and I was told they were fantastically good. In the book he wrote about it he unfortunately theorized, and got mixed up in the occult: 7 is the mystic number etc., etc. He very nearly discovered the *rejilla* – he sensed it – but got it wrong. The moment mystic matters come in, things do go wrong, as with arithmetic. But the first part of his book – no theory – has a lot in it which is very good.

I read his and other books on the subject while my own book was going to press. Apart from Lopez, most of the stuff was nonsense.

I was delighted to learn that you too had enjoyed *Now Voyager*, and that lovely Max Steiner music. My father used to say that Max Steiner was the writer for the films. For some reason he did not care much for Korngold; I think he felt that Korngold's music was 'contrived'.

What you wrote in your letter about musical snobbery was, to my mind, absolutely exact, and your analysis of how it spread until it even reached audiences is masterly. The worst moment (it ended by influencing all Europe and America) was when the snobs established their 'cell' in the BBC. Stravinsky, in his autobiography, went into raptures about the wonderful young men in the BBC who 'really understood' music; but then he was one of the beneficiaries, the more so as his music became more tortuous. I don't think the 'wonderful young men' cared much for *L'Oiseau de Feu* or *Petrouchka*.

One of the things which struck me very much at the time was that a number of composers who could have written melodic music did not have the courage to do so. And the music academies killed potential composers, as the art schools killed young artists. In the early 1960s, when for a brief period I lived in London, I knew two young men, an English composer and a Chinese artist. Both were wrecked by music and art school respectively – in one year. The composer never wrote another note, and ended as a schoolteacher; the artist, who should have been studying anatomy and mastering the nude, produced formless muck, lost all individuality, and vanished from the art world, goodness knows where.

Both, while studying, used to come and play or show me their work, which each time became more shrivelled and dried up. I said to the composer, 'Play me the work you played to me last year.' He smiled rather loftily, and declined, saying the work was 'very juvenile'. 'Maybe it was,' I said, 'but I remember it.' No effect at all. The mind had been closed – by a music school.

My father once said to me that, with Richard Strauss and Ravel, music had reached a point beyond which there was nowhere else to go. (He was thinking in terms of orchestra, of course – as he always did.) His view was that in the next century – which seemed very far away when he said it – music would have to go back to its very simple beginnings, and start all over again. Another of his injunctions was that all students of composition should be required to write a four-line hymn tune once a week – a four-line hymn tune being, in his opinion, the most difficult of all forms of composition, in that it reveals to the student his every fault, and is thus the most useful way of learning.

He also said that the last three notes of a melody are the most difficult, in which a composer who is not really first rate will reveal his weakness. This is undoubtedly true, and all the great symphonic composers have tried to avoid ending a melody. Songwriters were not so lucky; they had to. If I had to award a laurel for tune ending, it would go to Franz Léhar. It is terribly difficult to make the last notes of a melody convincing. For this reason, composers make the tune go up at the end, then down. Léhar very seldom had to do this, Johann Strauss too very seldom, except for comic effect. Theirs were what I call natural melodies.

But reverting to my father, there was a comic side to this, to which, out of filial obedience, I never referred. While almost revering Massenet, he paid only cursory attention to Bizet, which always seemed to me to be extraordinary, until it dawned on me that Bizet wrote one – I repeat one – bad ending: the 'Toreador's Song' in *Carmen*. That, for my father, was enough.

Almost equally funny was the fact that – and again I think it was concerned with tune endings – he could not stand Offenbach. With his scrupulous attention to music, he simply could not take it in that Offenbach used bad endings to convey comedy. My father appreciated the joke, but did not like the manner of it.

This is rendered even stranger by the fact that Offenbach produced – in 'Elle a fuie, la tourterelle' – the song of all songs, with a perfect ending, but which does not end. You could go on singing it for ever. The only other song I can think of which does the same thing is the Welsh song 'David of the White Rock', which Edward German brought so beautifully into his 'A Welsh Rhapsody'. (I insisted on this work being played at my father's centenary concert in Nottingham, with the Royal Philharmonic Orchestra.)

I feel sure that you must have heard Victoria de los Angeles singing 'Elle a fuie, la tourterelle'. For me, it was one of the most wonderful sounds I ever heard in my life, singing what is probably the world's most perfect song. Her perfect French enunciation – so difficult and so rare – only made it seem lovelier.

A thought occurs to me. It may be *fui*, not *fuie*. Having always regarded French as my own language, but seldom having to write letters in it, I make frightful grammar mistakes. (So do French parish priests, from the pulpit.) Please carry on.

While on the subject of Victoria de los Angeles, her perform-ance of *Manon* – Massenet's *Manon*, which I have on record – is incomparably the greatest performance of France's most difficult opera that has ever been made. Beecham said that *Manon* was probably the most perfect opera ever written. It is one of the most difficult operas to stage. I once saw – at the Coliseum in London – a perfectly staged performance. But it did not have a *Manon*. My remembrances of *Manon* go back to the 1930s, with Albert Wolff conducting at the Opéra Comique.

With Victoria de los Angeles, on record, one has the most astonishing performance of *Manon* which has ever been given. Lim Chong Keat, the greatest architect in south-east Asia, himself a friend of Victoria de los Angeles and one of her greatest admirers, said to me, 'Did you notice how between Act One and Act Two she'd been raped?'

Of course I'd noticed. I'd never heard anything like it in my life – the controlled change in the calibre of the voice. Nothing like this has ever been done in opera – and recorded.

A great deal is said of Maria Callas. I have myself witnessed some of her great performances, above all as Tosca. She had a limited range, however, and would never for a moment have survived outside the Italian net. She had only three vowels on which to sing.

There are so many things I want to tell you. I somehow think that Mercedes will understand. Please give her a big hug from me, and from a lower level (but only slightly lower) Yim. And being the official photographer is not that silly. One never knows, 130 years from now.

This year, however, we seem to be stuck, Yim's Spanish visa having run out. Short of going back to Hong Kong, there is no possibility of getting it renewed. We are therefore confining our journeys this year to inside Portugal, although sometimes very close to Spain. On Monday 2 July we shall be at Marvao, perched high up on an amazing hilltop, of vital importance during the Roman period, and which my cousins say I have got to visit. Gerald, in fact, will be driving us there.

Lim Chong Keat will be coming the week after that to stay with us, and so will Angela Ling, utterly beautiful and the representative of McDonald's hamburgers (heaven help us, but never mind, I don't care what my friends do so long as it's productive).

Yim says will I please tell Mercedes that Verde, the bird with whom she was photographed, is now a father. Cinzento – rather aloof at the time of your visit – turned out to be Cincenta, laid five eggs, and has hatched two. Amarelo – or Amarela? one never knows – refuses to come out of the nest box, and Cincenta insists on going on feeding him/her, driving Verde nearly mad. He is so angry; it is one of the funniest bird situations we have come across.

Dearest love to you both, and there are so many things I want to say but haven't.

Very affectionately,

Austin

————⚬⚬————

Monte Carlo, End of August 1990

Dear Austin,

Eventually I am able to thank you – and very much indeed – for your long and fascinating letter of last June. I was delighted and thought, when it arrived, of writing back immediately, but the last weeks before holidays, which are usually very busy, have been this year especially so. We came here late July and, again as usual, had to sort out quite a number of papers that were awaiting me. I'm sure you know this matter so well.

I cannot thank you enough for having so kindly done my numbers. When you write 'I would have said that you would be musical, but would have probably left it at that', I think you shrewdly hit the nail on the head. For, after all, I did leave it at that myself, having done nothing of musical importance in my life. Probably the truth is that I have always had a passion divided between music and letters, becoming at the end neither a musician nor a man of letters. (Touching a little bit of both, perhaps, I wrote a book years ago, *La Sociedad Filarmónica de Bilbao*, a kind of history of this very old, and very dear to me, philharmonic society).

It amuses me that you mention the dance band leader, Lopez, as a remarkable numerologist. I believe he was Francis Lopez – at least he came to Paris and was famous as Francis – and wrote very second-rate (were they third-rate?) songs for a second-rate popular Spanish singer whose name was Luis Mariano. Apparently Francis Lopez became a very wealthy man and so did his widow, Anja Lopez, who was extremely popular in Monte Carlo until she died, two or three years ago, plunging into the sea with her helicopter and her lover. (By the way, on one occasion I shared with her a helicopter between Nice and Monaco... with much better luck. Incidentally, it was around eleven in the morning and she looked like a jeweller's window!)

But, coming back to the numerology subject, I quite agree with you: there must be something in it, although all of it is most uncanny. How can a name, cast capriciously upon somebody, affect or influence his or her life?

I was very glad to learn that your father considered Max Steiner, the writer of film music, so highly. He was indeed such a marvellous composer. I don't know whether you have come across the relatively new recordings of the original music for the movies conducted by Charles Gerhardt. They were produced by George Korngold (son of EWK) and made by RCA in America. They are a very good proof, if any were needed, of the fine quality of that music written by M Steiner, E W Korngold, B Hermann, A Newman and F Waxman during the Hollywood golden years. (Please tell me whether you know these recordings or not, for I can easily get some of them for you. I'm sure you'll enjoy them very much.)

On the other hand, it certainly surprises me that your father did not care much for Korngold. I must confess I am a great admirer of his music, specially the astonishing 'Sinfonietta' op.5 he wrote when he was only fifteen years old!

I entirely agree with your opinion of Stravinsky's music and the 'wonderful young men' in the BBC. Following the pattern of stock exchange reporters, I would say that he reached an all time high with *L'Oiseau de Feu*, and paradoxically he came down from that peak little by little – becoming more and more tortuous, as you said – until his end. Was he also jealous of the attention the musical snobs were paying to the Vienna School composers?

How right your father was about R Strauss and Ravel. A friend of mine firmly believes that *Daphnis et Chloë* is the most inspired work in the entire history of music. I don't know myself if this kind of statement can be made at all, but Ravel's music is certainly something that seems really unsurpassable. One is left speechless in awe before such a genius.

What you wrote – and your father maintained – about songs with good or bad endings is fascinating. I never thought of a good or bad ending technically speaking. I felt, of course, whether a melody ended convincingly or not, but without realizing it happened according to certain established rules or principles. I'm determined to pay much more attention to this matter in the future. (*En tout cas*, when I get back to Madrid, I will record some of my favourite songs on a cassette for you. It will let you know my predilections, and also my weaknesses.)

I do have the Victoria de los Angeles records you mentioned. In fact she is too one of my favourite singers and I do share your opinion about her singing of 'Elle a fui, la tourterelle' and the beauty of this song. The rest of *Les Contes d'Hoffmann*, though, with the exception of the lovely 'Barcarolle' does not appeal to me very much, although I cannot give any good reason. You certainly made me feel curious about the Welsh song, 'David of the White Rock' and German's 'A Welsh Rhapsody', for I have never heard either of them. In fact I think the first time I heard of Edward German at all was when I was reading your father's autobiography.

Going back to Victoria de los Angeles, I have been very lucky to have listened to her in many recitals, especially in her good years when she came frequently to sing at the Sociedad Filarmónica de Bilbao; – but alas! – never singing in opera.

There is a lot I'd like to tell you about *Manon* and *Werther* but then this letter would never reach Colares. One thing, however, I don't want to forget to mention. Although I said I did not think before of how good was a song ending, I did consider many times this point concerning books, both fiction and non-fiction. I feel it's more important, of course, in the former.

I have started rereading those of your books I read before we met, for now I read them with 'different eyes'. And I believe that *Myself a Mandarin* is a clear instance of what I said before: a book with a marvellous ending. In fact the whole narrative has a sort of musical rhythm, carrying the reader to the last and very moving story. I could see myself the sad and intense look of the young girl and felt almost the same you felt yourself. I could also see the detached way the Special Magistrate passes the turnstile – by the way, now it is 1HK dollar instead of 10 cts – and crosses the harbour to the airport. I could almost feel his mood when he looks down from the plane window, thinking of the crabs he had been promised for midnight supper in Singapore…

I have really enjoyed this second reading of your book, much more than the first, which is only natural, for then I hadn't met yet the Special Magistrate.

It is a great pity that this matter of Yim's Spanish visa has prevented your coming to Madrid this year. Mercedes and I were very much looking forward to your visit. Actually, when I saw June advancing into July without news from you I thought that something negative had happened. Unfortunately, I don't know whether I'll be able to see you in Portugal before you leave. Our plan is to be in Madrid the first week of September. Then I have a tight programme of customers' visits. Anyway, I will telephone you when I am back in Madrid. When are you going back to Hong Kong? I might be there myself in October.

Mercedes sends you her love. By the way, she was delighted with the story of her friend, 'Verde'.

My best regards to Yim and all my best to you,

Yours ever,

Ramón

PS When I was in Hong Kong last May I bought *Quick Tidings*, fresh from the printers and I thoroughly enjoyed it. It's really admirable the way you can turn any subject into the most attractive book. How is the history of Portugal going on?

Colares, 22 August 1990

Dear Ramón,

I had been hoping to come to Madrid after the hot weather, and have now realized that Yim's Spanish visa has run out and there is no way of extending it except by going back to Hong Kong first – he travels on a certificate of identity issued by the Hong Kong Police, and a Consul can only put a 'chop' on it in Hong Kong. So this means putting off a visit till next year.

Forgive me for writing such a long letter last time, but it was in reply to three of your own, all very interesting, and even in ten pages I did not have space to say everything, such was my delighted surprise to learn that you had had associations with Plantation House. You spring one surprise after another.

I am spending the months here in a wide range of reading, thinking about my proposed short history of Portugal, and generally having cold feet about it. A history of a nation is a depressing subject, especially of this one, with its centuries of ignorance and superstition. But perhaps I shall in the end see a way round the depressing side of it. Professor Charles Boxer says to me, 'Just start, and you'll find it'll be all right.' But I still have only one toe in the water.

Please give my love to Mercedes. I assume you are in Monte Carlo at present.

Very dear regards as ever,

Austin

————————◦○◦————————

Madrid, 15 September 1990

Dear Austin,

This is the story I promised to you. It all began this summer at Villeneuve-les-Avignon. I don't know if you have ever visited this charming little village that looks at Avignon from the west bank of the Rhône river. It has, for me, two main points of attraction: Le Prieuré and La Chartreuse. Le Prieuré is a delightful hotel. It is specially so during summertime, for then the restaurant tables are laid in a lovely yard, under very old trees. The air is clean and the only smell is that of flowers and tree-leaves. Put an extremely fine cuisine on top of that and you will have the whole picture.

La Chartreuse is a big compound – from the thirteenth century, I believe – the biggest Carthusian monastery in Europe, I was told. Anyway, it consists of a beautiful group of buildings and yards and in one of these, on August the first, our friend Ruggero Raimondi was giving a *Liederabend*. So there we went, and now I come to the point. During the dinner that followed the music I talked to Ruggero about your father's music, especially about his songs. He was very interested, and when we travelled together to Funchal last weekend, I gave him photocopies of some songs – the ones in the *Chappell's 100th Anniversary Edition* – and a cassette copy of the CD recorded by Brian Rayner Cook, *The Songs of Eric Coates*. I am afraid I broke the copyright law in both cases but it was the only way of introducing RR to EC's music. Will you forgive me?

After looking at the music he said he will probably sing some of them next January in Madrid. Isn't that wonderful? The great pity is that by then you will be on the other side of the planet.

Our visit to Madeira left us a bit disillusioned with this island. Perhaps our expectations were too great and the reality didn't match up to them. Of course, there were, as usual, good and bad points. The worst of these was the miserable weather, almost non-stop raining. I did enjoy, though, recalling the opening of your *A Macao Narrative*, for in Funchal there is not only an Avenida do Infante, but a beautiful statue of Henry the Navigator. I took a photograph of it for you. I hope it doesn't come out too badly. There is also an *avenida* named after Miguel de Arriaga. Next time I will tell you why I'm very much interested in this Arriaga.

I'll do my best to see you next weekend in Colares. If so, I will probably be there sooner than this letter. But one never knows, so I'll post it tomorrow. (I'll contact you by telephone, anyway.)

Looking forward to seeing you next week,

Yours ever,

Ramón

Madrid, 31 October 1990

Dear Austin,

Over the last two days – well, as a matter fact, the last two evenings – I have dialled your telephone number in Colares several times, but you were not in. This morning I have telephoned again, this time both your Colares and Hong Kong numbers without getting any reply. So I assume you have departed earlier than expected and are travelling somewhere on your way to Hong Kong.

It's a great pity that some unlucky circumstances have prevented our seeing each other during this year.

Shortly after we spoke last time I went to the Far East, spending some days in Taipei and then in Hong Kong. Just by chance I happened to be in Taipei for the celebration of the Double Tenth and I was really astonished at the sight of the thousands and thousands of ROC's flags waving everywhere. It was also amazing to watch the crowds at the Generalissimo's Memorial, paying their respects before his godlike statue. How long is all this going to last? I very much enjoyed a visit to the National Museum – even though it too was very crowded – admiring its many treasures. Robberies, as the Peking's government claims?

In Hong Kong, to commemorate the first hundred years of China Light Company, they have decorated some streets around Statue Square, especially Chater Road, with numberless lights. At night thousands of bulbs draw the shape of the Legislative Council building, the Hong Kong Club and many others, besides reproducing some Chinese decorative motifs on several façades. It really was a fascinating spectacle and I very much hope the lights are still on when you arrive. I'm sure you will enjoy strolling one evening from Chater Road eastward.

Talking of matters of consequence – as the Little Prince would complain – I did not perceive in Hong Kong any particular change of sentiment among the people I could talk to. So much is in the air, including, in my opinion, very much wishful thinking. Which seems only natural, one can blame nobody for that. After all, who knows what may happen to that Old Guard in Peking before 1997, and to China for that matter?

With this letter I enclose a photograph I took in Funchal. As you can see, the man represented in that statue is your 'good friend', Henry the Navigator, very properly portrayed gazing out across the sea and into the far distance.

By separate mail I have sent to you one of those recordings made by Charles Gerhardt in 'The Classics Film Scores' series that I told you about. This one is devoted to the music of EW Korngold. Maybe after listening to it, you will share part of my admiration for Korngold's music.

Please let me know about yourself. Have you already followed your friend Charles Boxer's advice and started the history of Portugal? I agree with him, 'it'll be all right' – and I'm sure you will make it a fascinating reading, as you always do.

I look very much forward to seeing you somewhere, any-where. Please convey my kindest regards to Yim.

With great affection,

Yours

Ramón

PS I forgot to tell you that I have read Jan Morris's *Hong Kong* and found it uneven but parts of it quite interesting and attractive. Have you read it?

Hong Kong, 19 November 1990

Dear Ramón,

Thank you so much for your letter of 31 October and for the Korngold CD, which arrived two days earlier. We don't have a machine for playing CDs yet, but Yim is going to buy one this week, and I look forward very much to listening to the Korngold music. I remember all those titles as they came out. I couldn't get into a cinema to see *The Constant Nymph* because it was ADULTS ONLY; but I saw *Anthony Adverse* – lovely music – and *Escape Me Never*, which for some curious reason was not ADULTS ONLY.

I wanted to see *Escape Me Never* on the stage, but it was sold out solid – Elisabeth Bergner's perfect triumph. My mother saw it on the last night. When it was announced that it would be coming off, my mother put her foot down. My father telephoned Charles B Cochran, who was presenting it, and Cockie had one seat left in his special allotment. At least my mother was able to give us a fairly dramatic account of it afterwards.

The only reason I can think of for my father's strange reaction to Korngold was that he should have had the courage of his convictions and stayed in the concert hall. Yet why did he not have a similar reaction to Max Steiner? And how on earth, with all the musical snobbery, could Korngold – or Max Steiner – have remained in the concert hall? One popular success, and they would have condemned themselves to oblivion, or else the Boston Pops, if they could even have got in there.

Of course, my father, when speaking of Korngold – usually to brash idiots asking him why he didn't do the sensible thing and make some money – would never say anything except in praise of Korngold. He never spoke ill of another composer. And about the concert hall business, he had perhaps forgotten what he said to me, aged six, warning me never to be a musician: 'Remember, I am one in a million.'

You telephoned me at Colares at exactly the moment when we were neither there nor in Hong Kong, as you rightly deduced, and mentioned in your letter. We were actually in London. We left Colares on 28 October, and were in Hong Kong on 2 November. I'm so sorry that at neither end was I able to take yours calls. I have the same sense of regret that we did not manage to meet this year.

About Taiwan, I'm so glad you were there for the Double Tenth – though it must have been awful for doing any business – because in seeing that, you are actually seeing the real China. That is it, as a nation, with its flags and worship of monuments, its wonderful discipline when convention demands (its total lack of discipline otherwise, until arrested and thrust into prison), and its general feeling of the unreal.

It is the greatest black market for books, tapes, videos, music, anything you like to name – entirely legal, since China – the real China in Taiwan – did not sign the Copyright Conventions. It is not a black market at all, and we all love it. Yim and I will be going over in February, and will come back with a stack of books costing 20% of New York prices.

I know what you are saying. But, please, we are human.

Taiwan is China, the real China. Whether China in the future will once more fly the flag that is flown in Taiwan is uncertain. What is certain is that some day the present flag of China will have to be changed. To the Chinese people it is a symbol of horror. Only that remarkable discipline when convention demands, assures its place on the flagstaff.

Yes, I took Charles Boxer's word, and started. It did so with a bang, and it's very nearly right. At least I've got the beginning point right – those impossible half-sisters Urraca and Tareja. Heaven knows what will happen after this.

But I think I ought to have a look at Santiago, León, Zamora – then Madrid – and Badajoz, before going in again to Elvas in Yim's little car. God knows what the Ritz will say when we turn up in it! The man who has to drive it into the car park will feel so insulted, I can't wait to see his face. Upon his face, in fact, will depend his tip. This will probably happen in April.

You will, I assume, be in Korea, Japan, Taiwan, or possibly Barcelona. Therefore Mercedes, Yim and I will sort it out by telephone. Somehow we will meet.

Very dear regards to Mercedes and to yourself as always,

Very affectionately,

Austin

IV: 1991

Madrid, 24 January 1991

Dear Austin,

It's incredible how fast time flies. When we got back from London, well over a month ago, I had every intention of writing to you immediately... and it seems now that that was yesterday!

Around Christmas we (Mercedes and I) went north to Bilbao, and spent a few days seeing our families there, having too many parties and eating a bit too much, as usually happens at Christmas time. Then we came back to Madrid for New Year's Eve and saw the new year in very quietly at home. What about you?

When in London, we were invited to attend an extremely good concert, the programme of which I'm enclosing with this, since everything that evening had a sort of Portuguese flavour. As you will see, both the concert and the excellent dinner that followed were held to celebrate the Banco Espirito Santo's tenth anniversary in London and, very properly, the very fine Portuguese pianist Maria João Pires was the 'star' of the evening. I strongly recommend you to listen to some of her latest CDs of Mozart and Schubert – they are really superb. My feeling is, however, that because of those unimaginative bicentennial celebrations, by mid-1991 we won't be able to digest even the shortest of Mozart's works. As we say in Spanish, '*lo poco agrada, pero lo mucho enfada*' (I'm sure you can translate it very well).

Talking of music, Ruggero Raimondi gave his recital in Madrid but, disappointingly, he didn't include any of Eric Coates's songs in his programme. I did not dare to ask why at the time, but my guess is that he had not had the time to study and rehearse them. Nevertheless, I'll try to raise the subject with him in the near future.

Did you get the compact disc player? Have you already managed to listen to Korngold's music? I'm very much looking forward to hearing how you liked these spectacular new recordings of that music which, in films, often almost faded away.

And still on the subject of films, I would like to advise you not to miss the new Chinese film *Ju Dou*, if it is showing in Hong Kong. It is a strong drama, directed by the talented Zhang Yimou, with three first-class actors – including the beautiful Gong Li – and a marvellous photography. Maybe it was because I'm not accustomed to seeing Chinese films and therefore I lack enough references, but *Ju Dou* seemed to me a minor masterpiece.

I was very amused when I read in your last letter about *The Constant Nymph* being classified ADULTS ONLY. It made me recall my own childhood, when so many good films were out of my reach for the very same reason. Later on, when I saw many of them I was astonished and could not understand such stupid bigotry. Now everything is upside down and a boy or a girl of thirteen can watch really disgusting scenes – legally! This has probably something to do with the lack of good manners nowadays in our society, especially among the younger generations – at least in Western countries.

About Taipei and its black market for books etc., I too bought some books when I was there! By the way, if this letter arrives before you leave for Taiwan, I'd like to ask you a very special favour: to search for one copy of *Personal and Oriental* or *Invitation to an Oriental Feast*. Although they are out of print in Hong Kong and London, maybe you could find some 'illegal' copies in Taipei.

I'm more glad to learn of your plan to come to Spain (Madrid included). I'll certainly not be in the Far East, nor in Barcelona. I'll await with much pleasure your arrival in Madrid. If it is early May and we have finished some work we are doing in our flat, we should be very pleased to have you to stay with us. There is a guest room with two beds (sorry we haven't got two rooms) and a bathroom 'en suite'. Certainly it's not the Ritz, but we won't look down on Yim's little car... Anyway let me know about your dates and plans.

My very best regards to Yim.

Yours ever, with great affection,

Ramón

---o○o---

Hong Kong, 13 February 1991

Dear Ramón,

You said it was incredible how time passed, how you had resolved to write to me immediately. I, when I received your letter, was shocked to the roots. Months before, I had written to you to thank you for the Korngold record, and to say how much I enjoyed it, and how I agreed with you about his orchestration and great musicianship.

Except that I hadn't written it. It was one of those letters written 'walking up and down', possibly wine glass in hand.

'Yes, dear, I know,' said Allison Werner, an enchanting White Russian lady friend of mine. 'Letters written in the bath.'

What is one to say? Except thank you very much for the Korngold record, and I agree with you.

You and Mercedes sound as if you had a splendid Christmas in Bilbao. We spent a quiet one here – things are rather quiet here – then went to Manila for Rizal Day. I always rather dread it, yet in the end enjoy it. I clank about covered with medals, feel awfully silly, meet everybody – Salvador Laurel, Fidel Ramos, the President of the Senate etc., and above all 'the clan', the Rizal family. We ended up having breakfast at the Manila Hotel – the ceremony is terribly early, to coincide with the moment of Rizal's death. I don't suppose he would agree with it, but what is one to do?

Then, after the New Year, we flew down to Singapore, where Tan Kok Seng, who looked after me from 1959–1979, took us over. The first evening, I met my great-granddaughter, born in Connecticut. The family have always regarded me as Kok Seng's father (or a kind of father) and so it goes on like that. Chee, his son, who is named after my Chinese name, has called me Grandad from the day he could talk; and so Beverly is my great-granddaughter, and it is perfectly useless to argue.

Kok Seng then drove us on a 1200-mile journey in Malaya visiting old friends, accompanied by San (Mrs Liao San) whom you met here – great fun, and she's always at her best when travelling, especially with us.

One day I will introduce you to Tan Kok Seng's three-volume autobiography, *Son of Singapore*. It is lovely, easy reading, and made him a name to be played with in south-east Asia. Apart from anything else, it gives a closer and more accurate picture of me that will ever be conveyed by anyone. Derek Davies, prior to reviewing the third and last volume for the *Far Eastern Economic Review*, insisted that he meet Kok Seng first; he did not really believe that Seng could have written quite such a work. I invited him. 'But he's so self-centred,' Derek said, 'and how can he be so rude to you?'

Hard to explain. A Chinese who is not self-centred is not worth his salt; and what Derek took for rudeness was simply a Chinese saying what he thought. (I had the same trouble when introducing Kok Seng in English society. It took several years for them to understand that you talk to Chinese as you do to anyone else, and he talks to you likewise.)

We're not going to Taiwan after all – we're coming to Europe earlier than usual, 6 March to London – which brings me to my first two books and the possibility of pirated editions. I think I may be able to find copies, at least of one. But your letter made me read the second one – *Personal and Oriental* – and I have written by this same post to my London publisher suggesting that it is about time there was a reissue. Thank you so much for raising the subject. (The book, as I now see, gives a fantastically accurate picture of Asia as it was in 1952, just pulling itself out of imperialism.)

You mention the guest room. May Yim and I please come and be house guests? It would be much nicer than the Ritz. And will you please tell Mercedes that, whether with Kok Seng or Yim, we have a reputation of being visitors who are welcome the second time. (It is not every visitor who is.)

And this brings me to the last point in this letter. I have just this very minute – about two hours ago – decided that I'm not going to go on with my idea of a history of Portugal. Instead, I'm going to do something like those two first books of mine, which are me, and yet through me you see nations and people. I think this will be much better. It also gives me more freedom. Those books were greeted in London and New York with immense acclaim. In them I spoke about people in Asia. This is how I think I ought to speak about the Portuguese and their past. One way or another, I think it will be better this way. At least, it will be more personal – and this, with Portuguese, is essential, I think. (You know what I mean. It is a very difficult subject.)

But we are dying to get back there. Chinese New Year (tomorrow) is so strange. We haven't received a New Year card – there are usually hundreds – nor have we sent any. Even from overseas no cards have come. All is quiet and rather depressing – waiting, possibly, for the end. Or at least for our end – we, and what we represent. Meanwhile, I am told, young Europeans are having a marvellous time in four tiny little streets downtown (in Lai Kwai Fong). No Chinese, of course, except the waiters.

Telephoning this morning for tickets for Europe, I had the strange feeling that this place was no more for me. Even more strange: Yim felt exactly the same, and said so.

When we get back to Colares I will telephone you. I do not like this war in Iraq – still less what may follow, which may find Spain in the front rank of a combat which is all too old.

There are so many other things I want to say, but cannot for want of time and space.

Yim says a big kiss to Mercedes, which I add to.

Dearest love to you both,

Austin

Hong Kong, 19 February 1991

Dear Ramón,

Just a note to say with great regret that we have had to abandon our idea of coming to Madrid this year. Yim has collided with the Spanish clampdown on visas, which is much more severe than I thought.

He went to the Spanish Consulate-General yesterday to apply. Normally the issue of a visa takes one day. Since he does this every year, and has to have a visa for every country he visits except Portugal, he times this annual operation very well – Britain, three weeks; France, two days; Benelux, four days; Spain, two days etc.

Well, yesterday he learnt that he must furnish a bank guarantee, and that I must furnish two bank 'chops', and then both of us must file affidavits sworn before a Notary Public, who must in addition 'prove' my signature (how this is done I don't know). It also sounded to me as if the Notary Public was required to appear at the Consulate-General with us, but I'm not quite sure of this.

Now, from experience I know that the bank part of it alone is going to take at least four days, sometimes more, and heaven only knows how long the Notary Public will take. And we have only nine working days before we leave for London. To make it worse, this is the first week of the Chinese New Year, when everything is half-shut because so many people are away – including Notaries Public, as I discovered by telephoning round yesterday to find one. I didn't, which was a nice beginning. But it made me tell Yim to call it off, after I'd spoken to the Consul-General's secretary.

I should hasten to add that with both Yim and me they were very nice at the Consulate-General; but they have their rules. And Yim has to collect other visas in those nine remaining days.

It springs, I suppose, from that outburst last year – in Brussels? – about Spain being a transit for Moroccans and Algerians entering Europe illegally. The clampdown caused consternation in Latin America, I believe, and in the Philippines we certainly had a dishful of it. My host's sister-in-law and two elderly ladies of equally impeccable respectability had an appalling time in the United States trying to re-route their round-the-world tickets (never very easy to do) because their first stop in Europe was Madrid, and Spain wouldn't let them in. Instead they went directly to Rome, and being very Catholic they were very pleased in the end.

Another nice one was a young Filipino historian friend of mine who is working on Hispano-Philippine history, and has been reduced to centring his work on London instead of Madrid, because Spain wouldn't let him in either!

I don't suppose it will last for long, but it's rather tiresome while it does.

The absurdity of it is that Spain gains nothing from it financially. All the gains from these, the most expensive visas on earth, go to the banks and the lawyers, none of whom are Spanish.

I will telephone you when we get back to Colares, date as yet uncertain, but I want to get home soon. As always in war, I have a homing instinct, and home for me is Colares.

I don't like this war at all. In August last, Saddam set a trap for President Bush – as I pointed out to Yim on the morning it happened – and Bush stepped straight on it. The truth is that if one Arab country devours another it means nothing to the West. Now the West is hopelessly enmeshed in Arab affairs, which it does not understand; and the consequences are liable to be very grave.* The East will of course continue boldly on course. The East's passivity and quietness in regard to the war are a terrible warning to the West to leave the Arabs alone.

One good thing. We now travel from Hong Kong to London via the sensible route across China and Russia. It cuts four hours off that awful seventeen-hour journey.

Very dear regards to you and Mercedes, and we will be in touch.

Very affectionately,

Austin

*How amazingly perceptive he was.

Hong Kong, 28 February 1991

Dear Ramón,

When you mentioned the movie *Judou*, I simply failed to understand what you were talking about. I tried the name out on Yim; he too drew a total blank. The problem is that the title is spelt in 'pinyin', which neither Yim nor I can understand. With old Wade-Giles system I can fire off a name at Yim with enough accuracy for him to give a quick think and get it right in Chinese – meaning, with the right tones, so we know what the Chinese characters are. With 'pinyin' we are lost.

Three days ago, the *International Herald-Tribune* carried the story about *Judou* being nominated for an 'Oscar' in Hollywood, and how China, which will not allow the film to be shown, is doing everything it can to stop the nomination. (Such lunacy.) I dashed into Yim's room, where he was reading the *Tung Fung Jih Pao*, which would certainly carry the same story, and said, 'Search your paper till you find out the name of that movie Ramón was telling us about!'

In less than two minutes he was back in my room. The movie is *Kuk Tao*, meaning 'Chrysanthemum Bean' – a terrifying name, relating to the child in the story. In Wade-Giles Mandarin it is *Chü T'o* – much clearer than 'pinyin', which is merely the slovenly Peking accent, put into rather slovenly English. Wade-Giles, based on French, works.

But is this not a fascinating example of how difficult it is for the East and West to be quite sure they are talking about the same thing? If I had been able to go into Yim's room and say '*Chü T'o*', it could be taken as certain that he would have given a little cough, then got it.

As it was, neither of us got it. So much for 'experts'!

I have discovered two copies – I mean one of each – of *Invitation to an Eastern Feast* and *Personal and Oriental*. I will bring them with me to London next week, and have them posted to you when we reach Lisbon. I am in fact just about to take soundings in London about their reissue. It's a question of timing, really – political timing, one might say.

The Iraq war ended this morning with both sides claiming victory. It reminded me faintly of the war between Siam and Cambodia. Both erected a Victory Arch.

With very affectionate regards,

Austin

PS Actually, we missed '*Judou*'. We were away in Malaysia. I don't think it ran more than a few days here; serious films never do.

———————o◯o———————

Colares, 16 April 1991

Dear Ramón,

It was so good to hear you and Mercedes on the telephone last month, and I hope the business problems you mentioned are sorting themselves out.

I am sending you my first two books under two separate covers, and by registered post, meaning that you will probably not receive them till after this letter. But I thought I ought to make a brief comment on them. I am already moving towards getting them reissued; politically the time is not right at present (too Arab), but it may become so; and then I shall have to preface each book with a short statement about dates (years), so that the reader knows where he is.

Invitation to an Eastern Feast was published in 1953. It deals with India 1944, prime time of the British Empire with no possibility of Indian independence; Burma 1945; and China 1949.

At the time of writing, I did not want to date it; and since much of the content is timeless the date didn't matter. With the second book, *Personal and Oriental*, again the date did not matter, because the conflict between communism and mental freedom was the same in 1957, the date of publication, as it was in 1952, the date of the journey across Asia which the book describes.

One reason why I have been so slow in sending them is that I have been rereading them myself. Because of the turmoil of takeovers in the London publishing world – ten years of it – there is no one left with any knowledge of the books their companies actually produced. I therefore need to be conversant when 'reminding' them.

The Chinese movie banned in China, with the incomprehensible name in Western spelling, has, as I suspected it would, arrived late in Lisbon – so convenient – and so we shall be going to see it. Here it will run, which in Hong Kong it certainly didn't.

It would take a great deal to make me shut my ears to the music of Mozart, but I am getting very near it. There was a Vivaldi revival some years ago; Radio Hong Kong has been playing Vivaldi ever since, everything they can dig up. It has gone on for so long, and with such vehemence, that at mere sound of Vivaldi's music – I don't care what it is – I switch off.

There is no real cure for this kind of mistreatment of music. And what it is one to say? Even 'Rose, Rose, I love you' was quite a nice little tune when it was first written.

Very dear regards,

Austin

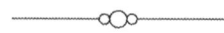

Colares, 19 April 1991

Dear Ramón,

I delayed sending this second volume because I wanted to put a note in it.

The journey it describes – from Japan to Turkey, meeting and staying with friends – was made in 1952, April to November. Rereading it myself, the impression it gives of Asia in 1952 is uncannily correct, possibly because I did not start writing it till three years later, so that the objectivity is there.

Underlying everything, of course, was the frightful and extremely dangerous struggle to resist communism, with which so much of my life has been concerned. I deal with it indirectly, my activities as a writer in those days being governed by the King's Colonial Regulations, the operative one – No. 7, I seem to remember – reading, 'An officer may publish anything of general interest, provided it appears under his own name, and does not concern politics or administration' – or words to that effect. It was the permissive phrasing of this regulation which caused me to accept Colonial Service appointment when it was offered.

In the Japanese chapter one sees Japanese contempt for the Russians, interesting today, and not understood at all by the world press. Russia will never forget 1905, and Japan will never forget 1945 and the tens of thousands of Japanese who were herded off to Siberia and never heard of again.

In the Chinese chapter one sees how the real issue was communism versus the Catholic Church, which was the strongest and the only true anticommunist force, because the struggle was basically doctrine versus doctrine.

I was amazed, reading the Philippine chapter, to see how much more Spanish the country was in 1952 than it is now. The decline in Spanish influence is a pity, because the country greatly needs the steadying influences of Europe. The American influence is essentially unsteadying. 'Doming's' father, referred to in relation to Spain, was the late Dr José Bantug, to whom General Ramón Blanco y Erenas gave his sword of honour in warrant of the truth of his statement that if he had been Governor General in December 1896 he would never have allowed Rizal's execution.

Again in the Philippine chapter there is a section called 'A village barber', in which I compare standards of living in various Asiatic countries. Filipinos never believed me at the time, whenever I told them they had what most others would call an enviably good standard of living. Reading this again I was quite shocked, because what was true in 1952 is not true any more. This winter, when I was in Manila, not a day went by without someone saying to me, 'We were once in the forefront. Look how we sent contingents to serve in the Vietnam War. And now look at us! We've fallen behind all the others and become a backward country.' I suppose part of the blame for this lies with Ferdinand Marcos, although not much. They're not really a backward country; they're just disorderly.

I see that I stated that Burma would never be a communist country, and by luck I have been borne out. But I never expected that Ne Win, admittedly an unpleasant man, would prove to be so persevering a dictator.

The short section dealing with Basra and Baghdad is as true today as it was then, except that in today's conditions it is not so easy to see. And for this present business of helping the Kurds, the Western nations are stepping into a bottomless pit. As any Iraqi will tell you, the Kurds cannot be helped. Whatever policy is pursued towards them, there will be rebellion of one kind or another. In 1952 the Kurds were in rebellion in both Iraq and

Turkey. They are always in rebellion, and for this reason they are regarded simply as a nuisance, not a real issue.

The decline in Spanish cultural influence in the Philippines was a subtle thing. Spanish was spoken really only by the upper echelon of society, and by the Church in private, i.e. priests talking among themselves. By the mid-'50s, when the country was finding its feet as an independent nation, speaking Spanish outside home acquired a snob aspect which most people didn't like. It had become the private language of the rich – entirely by accident. In the Church, evidently by policy, the personnel changed. By the 1960s the Jesuits were virtually an American Order, and so were even the Dominicans. The result of all this was that my young historian friend in London, who belongs to a wealthy and powerful family, but not an 'old' family, had to learn Spanish as a foreign language.

It is fascinating in the 'old' families, who speak an unconscious mixture of Tagalog, Spanish and English, that when saying anything subtle and personal or something expressing a judgment or assessment of something, it comes out invariably in Spanish.

Also, when talking to each other on the telephone – extending an invitation, for example – Spanish is the friendly language, English is a bit stiff, and Tagalog isn't quite right.

Another identification occurs to me. Don Evaristo (page 153) was José Laurel, President of the Philippines in the Japanese period, whose son Salvador Laurel is today's Vice-President.

In the next bit, Eugénio – believe it or not – was the key Filipino scientist in the team which created 'miracle' rice, which doubled India's rice production.

As ever,

Austin

Madrid, 26 April 1991

Dear Austin,

Today has been a very happy day for me: this morning your copy of *Invitation to an Eastern Feast* has arrived, and I am delighted. It is awfully kind of you and I want to thank you very much indeed. It does look very promising.

It has also made me take, at last, my pen and, rather ashamedly, get down to writing to you in reply to your letters of last February. In fact, I was doing this when weeks ago you very kindly telephoned from Colares. Then, after we had spoken, the letter I was writing was no longer the one I wanted to mail to you, so I tore it up. Thus I had no letter to take to the post, but I did have (and still do) too many troubles in my office, which are the only excuse for my having delayed so long writing this.

I was very happy, as usual, when I got your letters so full of news. Both Mercedes and I were absolutely delighted when we thought you were coming to Madrid and staying with us, so it was a great disappointment when your second letter arrived telling the sad story of Yim's collision with the present Spanish rules on visas. I had no idea at all that the situation could be like that, and it surprises me that, after all, we receive so many tourists from non-EC countries.

Anyway, the real trouble is that visa problem which is going, once again, to prevent your coming to Madrid. Therefore a possible trip for us to Portugal remains our only chance of seeing each other this year. I would very much like to do it and I do hope we'll be able to, but at the moment I cannot say when.

To start with, I'm awaiting a new car. The old Rover was giving me so many headaches that I finally decided to get rid of it at any price. Enough is enough. Now I have changed my new car's nationality – I'm sorry to say – and next month I'm going to take delivery of a Mercedes-Benz. It can definitely be a nice 'excuse' to travel again to Cascais and visit you sometime during the summer. I'd really love to do it.

As I said before, however, I have several problems to cope with in my office, which are very unpleasantly complicating my life. It is not at all easy to run a business in Spain nowadays – at

73

least some businesses – and the prospect of the European Single Market horrifies me. But *c'est la vie*, I suppose, and one simply has to be brave enough to accept rain or sunshine as a matter of course.

Now, as I write, I am under a sort of sunshine, for I'm listening to my latest discovery, some songs written by the Argentinian composer Carlos Guastavino. There is one, 'La Rosa y el Sauce' (the Rose and the Willow) which is really intoxicating. I have a recording made by the great Spanish mezzo-soprano, Teresa Berganza, and I never get tired of listening to it, time after time. Have you ever heard of Guastavino?

The story of your good friend Tan Kok Seng is fascinating, and I congratulate you for having met your great-granddaughter, Beverly. What you said of Tan Kok Seng's three-volume autobiography has me looking forward to reading it. Obviously only a self-centred person is prone to write a three-volume autobiography! Arthur Rubinstein only wrote a two-volume one, being himself both extremely charming and quite self-centred. What would Derek Davies have said of Sir Compton Mackenzie's ten-volume (!) autobiography? What really amazes me is that Sir Compton decided, when he was eighty, to write his autobiography in ten volumes, at a pace of one volume per year – and he did it! Quite a remarkable man!

The decision you have made about your book on Portugal seems to me both a pity and a brilliant idea. It's a pity we are not going to have your history of Portugal. On the other hand, I'm already looking very much forward to seeing Portugal, its past and its people, through your eyes, through yourself. I entirely agree with you, it will not only give you more freedom to write, but it will have a greater appeal for the general reader as well, and therefore will certainly be much more widely read.

Next week I am flying to Dublin to attend a piano competition. I have been invited by my Japanese friends, who organize or sponsor it, so it will turn out to be, I hope, a not unpleasant mixture of music and public relations work. Besides, I keep very good memories of some months – alas many years ago – I spent there. I really used to love Ireland and the Irish.

As we said, we'll get in touch as the summer approaches, and I will let you know our plans for it.

Mercedes joins me in sending very dear regards to you and Yim.

Yours ever,

Ramón

Monte Carlo, 14 May 1991

My dear Austin,

Shortly after I wrote you my last letter another delightful surprise arrived – *Personal and Oriental* – which you so kindly accompanied with a long note. I don't know really how to thank you for everything but I'm sure you do know that I do it with all my heart.

I'm here halfway through *Invitation to an Eastern Feast* and it seems to me unbelievable you wrote such a fine and profound book being not older than thirty. I must confess I do enjoy so much your inimitable writing style and admire that ability of yours to put into words those intimate feelings which, as they are sometimes very intense, are usually so difficult to express.

I'm enjoying reading and rereading it slowly. Things like 'the sweetness there is about those changes life brings to us wherein we pass gently from one world into another' fascinate me, for I have felt exactly that emotion although I would have never been able to put it in words.

But coming to the main theme of your book, I have to say that India has always been to me both attractive and intimidating. In fact, many years ago, I was in Hong Kong, and even had a ticket to fly to Delhi, but at the last moment I cancelled it. Exactly why, I cannot say. It probably had to do with some unconscious fear of finding something too unpleasant, something that might destroy my childhood dreams of India.

Anyway, whatever the reason, India, through your eyes and perceptions, is a delight to know.

I came here just to pick up my new car and plan to drive back to Madrid tomorrow.

Kindest regards to Yim and all the best to you.

Yours ever,

Ramón

PS Have you ever heard Richard Strauss's 'Metamorphoses'? It probably is a minor masterpiece, but enchanting nevertheless.

Madrid, 26 June 1991

Dear Austin,

I have just finished reading the second book – *Personal and Oriental* – on your fascinating travels and very personal experiences in Asia, about forty years ago. And it's difficult to say which one I have most enjoyed. You have the power of conveying your stories so vividly to the reader that he feels as if he is actually travelling with you to all those places and meeting all those peoples. I felt that especially when reading about places I knew beforehand, like Kyoto or Hong Kong. Your account of that memorable lunch with Uncle, Third Brother and your other Chinese friends in Cheung Chau is simply marvellous.

But what can I say that you don't already know? Except thank you very much indeed for those books which I'm certainly going to reread with great pleasure. They will occupy a very dear place in my small library.

Àpropos, have you already started working on your book on Portugal?

The summer has burst in on Madrid with full strength. Only two weeks ago it seemed we were just about in mid-spring, but now the heat is really difficult to bear. We would very much like to escape to the sea, but for the time being that is not possible.

I didn't tell you before, but those revamping works we were doing in our flat became, all of a sudden, a sort of mini-drama. A water pipe burst in the kitchen and, according to Mercedes' account, the water went out like the water jet in Lake Geneva. Anyway, the flood even reached the kitchen of our neighbours downstairs – poor fellows! To our great consternation we soon discovered that all the plumbing in the flat was very old and in rotten condition. There clearly was only one way out of that mess: to put in new plumbing and have a complete new kitchen from scratch. And this we did. Or rather, this is what we are in the process of doing. With luck we'll have everything almost finished next month, before leaving for Monte Carlo.

This means we won't be able to make our planned trip to Portugal before September; we are so looking forward to it. It is certainly our intention and our wish to visit you this year before the summer ends. I'll let you know how we can manage it.

With kindest regards to Yim, all the best to you.

As ever,

Ramón

★

Eventually we did manage to make the expected trip to Portugal in September. Curiously, driving there from Madrid through Extremadura, one cannot help noticing the absence of natural borders between the two countries, the landscape on one side being indistinguishable from that on the other. Only the centuries-old political division exists. On the 12th, after the convenient stop in Trujillo, we were again in Cascais. It had been unusually hot all the way down, and the refreshing breeze at The Albatroz was blissful.

Next morning, relaxed and restored, we drove under a clean blue sky to Colares. The beautiful narrow road snakes through the trees along the little *serra* of Sintra before dipping down into Colares. A few kilometres before reaching this small village – on a very sharp bend in the road – I noticed on our left what looked like an important property. Only the upper part of the house and some palm trees were visible, the rest of it and the garden being protected from the road by high walls, painted in grey. These ended in a beautiful ornament, leaning on a higher stone pillar on both sides of the black metal gate. What immediately drew my attention was the name of this property, clearly fixed on the right side of the gate: *Qvinta da Arriaga*. This awoke my interest, for I thought it might be connected with the Spanish composer, J C de Arriaga, whose life was then the subject of my special research. I knew about the Portuguese branch of this family. Manuel José de Arriaga was appointed President of the Portuguese Republic in 1911. One century before, Miguel de Arriaga was a judge in Macao, and a central public figure in the life of that enclave. I wanted to find out if the *quinta* was connected to this branch of the Arriaga family, but unfortunately, there was nothing I could do. The gate was firmly, almost inhospitably, closed. Later on, when we were with Austin, I asked him about the present owners of the house, but he could not be of any help. Probably the name of Arriaga didn't mean much to him, except of course the one belonging to Judge Miguel de Arriaga, whom he had mentioned a number of times in two of his books on Macao.

Passing through and leaving the lively centre of the village of Colares, we arrived almost immediately in the Rua das Horas de Paz; very peaceful and quiet indeed.

On the interior, however, the atmosphere was not so quiet; Yim, for one, was quite excited; both he and Austin greeted us warmly. As soon as we arrived, Yim brought out the chilled Raposeira which we all greatly enjoyed. Yim was, as a matter of fact, the 'star' of the day. He had cooked a really delicious Chinese lunch, which now I much regret not being able to describe in detail. What I do remember is that it was, according to Chinese etiquette, rather plentiful and made everyone happy.

Austin had a little surprise for me. It was the recently published Portuguese translation of his *A Macao Narrative*, with the title of *Macau – Calçadas da História*, which he had very kindly inscribed, 'To my dear friend, RR, with happy remembrance of his visit to Portugal, Sept. 1991, Very affectionately'.

In the afternoon, we decided to go on an outing and Austin suggested we might see the Cabo da Roca – reputedly the westernmost point of the European continent. I asked what was left of the Spanish claim to Cabo Finisterre as Land's End. Promptly, Austin produced a bulky atlas – luckily with latitude and longitude references – and there was no doubt left at all. Cabo da Roca was/is at longitude 9° 30' West of Greenwich. Finisterre at merely 5° 44' W. (We could verify of course that many points on the Irish west coast – non-continental Europe – fall more than 10° West of Greenwich).

Anyway, off we went to Cabo da Roca which is not far from Colares, and once again the photographs taken that day by Yim enable me to remember how after parking the car, we walked down to the lighthouse against a strong wind. Mercedes, Austin and I were laughing at our unruly hair when Yim, fast, took an amusing shot of us. The sky had totally changed since the morning and very dark clouds were approaching from the sea, an announcement of a summer thunderstorm. Early in the evening, we drove Austin and Yim back to Colares, as we had an appointment for dinner in Cascais with a Portuguese couple, very good friends of ours.

The following two days were rather hectic. We went to visit the beautiful Palacio de Queluz and its gardens near Sintra, and the huge but not so beautiful Palacio de Mafra, with its monastery and church sumptuously built of marble; both palaces dating from the first half of the eighteenth century. Austin was extremely happy reminiscing for us about Portuguese history and the lives of Dom Pedro III and Dom João V, which he knew so well. We went to see Ericeira, and its spectacular beach where the sea was roaring and breaking with full force, and where I could take some of the best photographs of that trip. We ate in a typical local tavern in Colares and then went back to a nice dinner at Porto de Santa María, in Guincho. We really did a lot, and by the morning, when we left Cascais, were almost exhausted. Afterwards in Madrid, it was a few weeks before I could write again.

★

Madrid, 10 October 1991

Dear Austin,

I'm writing, as usual, later than I intended to do. But you know quite well how is life for us poor businessmen. As soon as I set foot back in my office I was caught in that sort of unavoidable trap which physically and mentally takes hold of me. I actually did a lot of work and travelling after Cascais – last week I was in Düsseldorf with my Japanese friends (and some Germans too) – and as your White Russian lady friend would have said, I wrote to you many 'letters in the bath'. Now, at last, I'm doing the real thing. And first of all, I would like – if I find the words – to thank you so much for the few wonderful days we spent together, for your very warm hospitality and for that something so difficult to define which makes one feel very happy. Maybe it is that rare commodity, true friendship. With these lines you will find enclosed some photographs taken either by Yim or by myself which I hope will make a good souvenir of our lovely excursions to Queluz, Ericeira and Mafra. I also took some of them in Colares, while drinking vinho verde and Raposeira, and enjoying Yim's delicious Chinese food.

I have given much more thought to that problem of yours – tribulation, you said – and I'm more and more convinced that you are really far from having said everything you have in store. And it is not only that book I suggested about Hong Kong – *Hong Kong Portraits, The Hong Kong I Knew* or whatever the title may be – which I'm sure would delight so many of your readers (me for one). With a life such as yours, so rich with kaleidoscopic experiences, I firmly believe you still treasure many fascinating books in your head. I do honestly think so. Please do not stop.

Some good news. If nothing unexpected arises, I'm planning to be in Hamamatsu (Japan) at the end of November, probably the weekend from 23–25, returning to Europe via Hong Kong. Could we meet again there? I'll let you know my exact dates.

With very best regards to Yim,

Yours ever,

Ramón

PS Mercedes sends her love to you both.

Colares, 22 October 1991

Dear Ramón,

Thank you so much for your delightful letter of the 10th, and for the photographs, which make a lovely souvenir of your visit, which we had both looked forward to so much, and which we enjoyed so much when it actually took place. I was deeply touched by the two of you making that long journey really only to see us. But I believe you are right; ours is a special and spontaneous friendship. Your views and impressions I find so harmonious that I could never possibly answer any of your letters in detail, because I would simply be saying, 'I agree, I agree, I agree…'

First, your projected visit to Hamamatsu. I greatly regret that we will not be in Hong Kong when you pass through. Ten days after you left here, Yim was operated on for hernia, and this means three months of taking things very carefully. He's not even allowed to drive his car yet, though I'm hoping the surgeon will allow him to when Yim sees him tomorrow. The surgeon, Calado Correia, is a remarkable man, very fine on psychology. As he says, it's not driving the car that is dangerous; the danger is of something unexpected happening, and having suddenly to step on the brake. Similarly with air travel: you see your luggage coming round on those whirligig things, and by reflex action grab it. So no air travel for three months. Actually, my Gibbon cousins both have birthdays near Christmas, so we thought we'd stay for these and return to Hong Kong early in January.

The close-up photograph of Yim, incidentally, is one of the best ever taken of him. It shows the serious side of him, which is very difficult to catch. And the one of the plants and cactus on the windowsill is a gem.

I have been given a lot of thought to doing another book. At present I'm toying with the idea of something tied to the Vasco da Gama centenary (1998) and actually dealing with the colonial period in Asia, which the Indian historian and diplomat KM

Panikkar called 'the Vasco da Gama Epoch, 1498–1945', though I would bring it on into the present, since in some parts of Asia the colonial mentality is still with us – only just, thank goodness. The various centenaries, Macao's 400th (1957), the Infante's 500th (1960), and of course Columbus next year. It would enable me to wander about and reminisce. And it's no use running away from it, the good old story of Vasco's voyage, and Columbus and João II, and the Infante must be told. We have, as you know, reached the stage of 'the story of Vasco da Gama's voyage is so well-known that it need not be mentioned here'. How sick and tired I got of that sentence when I was doing my book on rubber! The number of things which people knew in 1910 which people in 1980 had never heard of was impressive. I myself had never read the story of Vasco's voyage until this year – except in Camões. Stories have to be retold, if only to restore their simplicity.

Anyway, I mentioned it last night on the telephone to a friend of mine who works for John Murray. She said it sounded like a Murray book – which was what I also had in mind. I explain it to you very badly. I've got a very untidy draft of Page One, which will probably go on for weeks, Page One being the disaster area. Unless it is right, nothing else will be.

Please excuse this working manuscript paper. It at least allows for spread. I hope everything goes well business-wise in Japan. I greatly admire your approach to the Pacific Rim problem – miles ahead of most European businessmen – and Germany. Isn't it strange? The Axis was, in one way, absolutely right; and today it is essential to be with it, not against it. It is the most powerful combination on earth, and the sole means by which Europe will retain relevance in the twenty-first century. USA flies too high, and in any case the world is not run on morals. Not of that kind, I mean.

With very dear regards to you both,

Affectionately,

Austin

———————oOo———————

Colares, 21 November 1991

Dear Ramón,

Under separate cover I am sending you Tan Kok Seng's three books of autobiography which you asked about. After your visit to Japan I hope you will enjoy them.

The other evening we opened two of the bottles of wine which you and Mercedes so very kindly brought us. We opened a white and a red. Well, Spain and Portugal are countries of good wine – I don't mind what the French say – but these wines which you brought us are quite exceptional. They seem to me to be in a category of their own, where taste is concerned. I have not come across anything like them in Western Europe, and I thank you very much for such a discerning present.

This morning at daybreak it was one degree centigrade and there was a little frost – quite an excitement for Yim and me.

All the very best to you both as ever,

Very affectionately,

Austin

———————oOo———————

Madrid, 20 December 1991

Dear Austin,

Thank you very much indeed for your last two letters and your beautiful present of Tan Kok Seng's three books of auto-biography, which I found here on my return from Japan at the beginning of this month. Now I have to explain why I wrote to you from Hong Kong [this letter is lost] saying I was already reading them. When I went to Düsseldorf in October I met a Japanese who works for Kawai in Singapore and was going back there two days later. I immediately thought of Kok Seng's books and what you said about them, only being available in Singapore. I thought too of your late return to Hong Kong this year so I asked my Japanese friend to try to get them for me. Which he did in surprisingly short time. Thus, when I took my flight to Hong Kong, Tan Kok Seng's books were with me. Now I keep one set here and the other one in Monte Carlo – where we went for a long weekend two weeks ago. So, again, thank you so much for sending them.

Talking of the autobiography itself it makes, as you said, fascinating reading, so spontaneously told and at the same time using such an economical and precise style. I cannot help feeling, however, that at moments he could have gone deeper into himself. But this is just a feeling, not a negative criticism. I can well understand his great success and I hope there will be perhaps some day a chance of meeting him personally.

It was a pity you were not in Hong Kong when I was there for a few days. Would you believe that I had some close friends living at 80 Macdonnell Road? Isn't this a small world? I say I had, for they have already moved to a nice apartment in Repulse Bay. They are Miguel Sancho, a Spaniard, and Lourdes, his lovely wife from Paraguay. One night they took me to a Cantonese restaurant in Wanchai – I can't remember the name, but it was very good – where I had, for the first time in my life, a delicious snake soup. Later on I was amused to read in one of Tan Kok Seng's books that the snake soup is one of the finest delicacies of wintertime Chinese cooking. I fully agree with that.

As a visitor in Hong Kong, one hardly notices any visible change, with the exception of course of public works and the never-ending rise of new buildings. Locals, however, do talk of noticeable changes in Hong Kong life and not all of them for the better. Happily, to me everything seemed as pleasant as ever, and I could enjoy again crossing the harbour with the Star Ferry – under a beautiful blue winter sky – or having a perfect dry martini at Captain's Bar.

One thing that made me sorry was the disappearance of the Bloomsbury Bookshop. Do you remember it, small, with a sort of romantic air, near D'Aguilar Street?

By the way, in Hong Kong I made a round of several bookshops looking for *Islands of the South* but in all of them I was told it was out of print. I understood, talking to Yim in Colares, that a reprint was already in the market. Am I wrong?

How right you are about stories having to be retold! And what a good idea to reminisce and wander about those 500 years. I myself have to confess that I haven't read anything about Vasco da Gama since my school days. And how right you also are about Page One being the disaster area! Sometimes I would say almost the same about the first paragraph of an article, or even a letter.

I have read, incidentally, Payne's *The White Rajahs of Sarawak*, a very interesting book that made me think a lot of your Sarawak period and long for a visit to the Dyak country. The various centenaries you mention in your letter made me remember José Rizal's first centenary in 1996 and think that it might be the right time to have your very fine biography of Rizal translated into Spanish and published in Spain. Do you agree? I'd be delighted to do it myself and would try my best to be *traduttore* but not *tradittore*. Almost nobody in Spain knows anything about Rizal, and I believe it is high time to change that situation. I'd try of course to find a publisher here. What do you think?

I hope Yim is completely recovered from his operation, and so does Mercedes, who joins me wishing both of you a very merry Christmas and all the best for the New Year... and always.

Looking forward to seeing you next spring in Spain,

Yours ever,

Ramón

V: 1992

Hong Kong, 19 January 1992

Dear Ramón,

Thank you so much for your letter, which awaited me on our return last weekend. I'm so glad you liked Kok Seng's books. I know what you mean about the lack of depth in places. The situation was that he was writing for young people, and his aim – without saying so – was to instruct, especially in the last volume. I felt the lack of depth too, but said nothing for fear of upsetting the flow of what he was doing. You and Mercedes would love him, incidentally; he's a most engaging and attractive companion.

Bloomsbury Bookshop has left that nice little shop, as you discovered, and has moved into one of the so-called plazas, where it no longer has a street frontage. I haven't managed to find it yet, but will one day. *Islands of the South* is definitely in print, but the distributors seem to be having difficulties with it; I'm going to see them this week, and try to get things moving. The reissue has been mishandled in England, I understand why, but can't quite see how to put it right. I will bring a copy when we come to Madrid, as we are absolutely determined to do this year. Yim has already made visa enquiries; the situation is the same as last year, but he's going to start early and plod on till he gets a visa. Anyway, it's better than Thailand, where he can't get in at all – because he was born in Vietnam!

Your idea of a Spanish translation of my Rizal biography, timed to appear in 1996, I found enthralling, as you may well imagine, and particularly the idea that you would do the translation yourself, which would be an incomparable asset.

But would you ever have the time? It's a long book, and I fear you would find it a great burden. If you could find time to do it, it would be ideal. As to publishing, we would be getting near the centenary of the loss of Cuba and the Philippines, when there are bound to be haunting thoughts in Spain, and some publications. Also, if necessary, I think I could obtain some financial backing for such an edition without much difficulty.

Yesterday being Saturday (not a day for mailing letters), I read the first half of the biography, thinking how it would read to a Spaniard, in Spanish. It tells things which are uncomfortable, particularly in the early footnotes; yet it seems to me that they are told without bias, reflecting Rizal indeed, who pointed out the defects but was profoundly pro-Spanish. The comparisons with British India also tend to give balance, as they were intended to.

Pursuing further, the first thing I should do is give or lend you a copy of the original first edition in hardback (I have one at Colares). Then comes the problem of reverse translation (Spanish-English-Spanish). From my Rizaliana at Colares, which is extensive, I could give you, typewritten with page indications, seven-eighths of all Spanish quotations in their original Spanish. This would have the advantage of showing how Rizal's Spanish matured from colonial to metropolitan (something I could not do in English), and give Paciano's letters in the original. These are utterly fascinating, showing the standard of higher education in the Philippines, and breathing in another world. Paciano's letters, to get the full flavour, are in fact untranslatable.

We then have to deal with Unamuno's tributes to Rizal, which obviously have to be in the original. For this we need a copy of Retana's *Vida y Escritos del Dr. José Rizal*, 1907, in which they appear as an Appendix, if I remember right. The National Library in Madrid may have a copy, or you may know of some way of obtaining one. If not, the Austrian State Library at Vienna almost certainly has one, and I could make arrangements to consult it.

Then we need a copy of Palma's *Biografía de Rizal*, Manila, 1949. Ozaeta's English translation is so good that I used it directly, but in this case we must have Palma's original words. I shall be going over to Manila next month – in connexion with a fourth edition of the biography – and will see if I can buy or borrow a Palma.

About the translation from Tagalog, I'm almost certain I've got Epifanio de los Santos' Spanish translation of Rizal's surviving

Tagalog poem. All the other Tagalog quotations are very simple, and can be taken directly from my English.

We then come to the Rizal-Blumentritt correspondence, which is in German, and which contains many of the finest and most revealing of Rizal's letters. If you would like to translate these bits directly from the German into Spanish I could lend you my Volumes V and VI of the *Epistolario Rizalino* (I have reason to believe that my six-volume set of this work is the only one in Europe). There you will find the Rizal letters in German in facsimile, with opposite them a Spanish translation which fails to capture the strength of what Rizal is saying (it is a senior student's translation, if you see what I mean), and this of course became even worse when biographers took to double translation, Spanish to English, in which the letters become simply insipid.

For this reason everything in German translation in the biography was done by me direct from the German. I would venture to say that my translations are so accurate – down to little archaisms of language in those days, i.e. 'needs must that I...' – that it would be safe to translate direct from my English into Spanish. In any case, coming to Madrid we could bring the volumes, and you could judge the thing for yourself.

I think I may have Máximo Viola's *Memoir* – in utterly lifeless Spanish, but it can't be helped. The one work which baffled me when writing the book was José Alejandrino's *La Senda del Sacrificio*. All attempts to find an original failed, and I had to use the English translation – senior student type again, done by his son. The present head of the National Library in Manila, however, is a close personal friend of mine, so we may move a step forward here, because I'm sure the book is there somewhere.

Now, this all sounds very complicated; but in fact it will not be. I would put the Spanish originals each on a separate sheet which could be placed in its appropriated place – each would be page-numbered – in the volume you were working from.

As for the illustrations, Filipinos will be so excited when they hear about it that one can count on the fullest support, probably with the Philippine Ambassador in Madrid (or better still, his wife) acting as the channel and getting things moving. On my side I can provide an engraved photograph of Rizal – the one used

as the frontispiece – in perfect condition. A good
illustrative material has come to light since I pt
together in 1967, and it so happens that the leading r
young generation – very active and scholarly – has become a close
friend of mine; I sometimes stay with his parents when in Manila.
The father is a very wealthy businessman and a lifelong biblio-
phile. But all of this could be dealt with nearer the time, if the
idea takes shape.

I very much hope it does. It is wonderful that you have
suggested it, and in my opinion it would come at the right time,
and be in a sense reassuring, because Rizal was an outstanding
example of what Spain could produce in her overseas provinces.

About coming to Madrid, would some time in the second half
of May be sensible? I would be able to get away from Colares at
any time from 16 May onward. June would also be convenient on
my side. May I leave it to you to suggest a date? You are far busier
than I am – my problem is merely overseas visitors, of whom the
first lot arrive on 9 May, and goodness knows how many more
there will be. I think that, whenever we come, we will come by
train or plane. I'm not wildly enthusiastic about doing quite such
a long journey in Yim's little car, reliable as it is.

My love to Mercedes, and with very dearest regards as always,

Affectionately,

Austin

★

When Austin wrote this letter I was in California. I had had to go
for a business trip to Los Angeles and took advantage of my
cousin Ramón Andreu living there to do some quick sightseeing
around the south of this enormous metropolis. He very kindly
drove me to San Juan Capistrano, a place I had always longed to
visit, although I cannot really explain why. Perhaps the title of an
old song – 'When the swallows come back to Capistrano' – was in
my mind, although I was not the only one thinking of those birds.
Probably the same song inspired the name – the Swallow's Inn –
of a country and western saloon and that of the French-Belgian

restaurant, L'Hirondelle. The present Mission building was almost a replica of the original, founded by Spanish missionaries – this having been long ago destroyed by an earthquake – but it seemed to keep its character and I found it attractive. Nearby (in a street called Camino Capistrano), we discovered a small book-shop – 'bookstore', they call it over there – with the appealing name of 'Room with a View'. But it was not only the name, the whole exterior was also engaging and we went inside. The owner, a charming lady, was brewing some coffee and kindly offered us a cup. The smell was irresistible and we accepted it at once; it was really delicious. Indeed it was for me a very lucky morning, for browsing about the second hand books, I found, just by chance, a first edition of Richard Mason's *The World of Suzie Wong*! It is still one of my favourite Hong Kong novels.

The little town of San Juan Capistrano was very quiet and peaceful, as was the road bordering the ocean when we drove back to Long Beach and Beverly Hills. The Californian winter sky was a pleasure to look at, clean and deep blue.

Austin's letter was awaiting me in Madrid, but there were not going to be more letters from him – as a matter of fact, from either side – for about four months. With the spring, Austin and Yim came back to London and Colares, and during April we frequently spoke on the telephone planning their next visit to Madrid.

They arrived by train on 16 May, late in the evening, after a tiring journey of nine hours. I went to welcome them at the station, and Mercedes had prepared a light dinner on our small terrace. They had brought and very kindly presented us with some beautiful Indonesian tablecloths, made of cotton in lovely colours and patterns. They were indeed a delightful gift. After a few drinks, and feeling relaxed, we went on talking till the small hours.

In his book *Remembering Mr. Maugham*, Garson Kanin wrote that he developed a system to remember impressions, questions, answers, opinions and conversations. It was 'to write things down' immediately. 'I have found,' he said, 'that if I begin to set down a conversation on the same day on which it took place, I can report large portions of it accurately. If sleep intervenes, the work becomes more difficult, often impossible.'

How greatly do I agree with this! How so many times I have thought of this when trying, without success, to remember my countless hours spent with Austin, and both of us talking of everything under the sun. However, as Elizabeth Bowen confessed, 'I could remember everything, but only as a silent movie, without words.'

Next morning, I discovered that in spite of the 'small hours', Austin was a very early riser, as well as early reader. When we woke up, Yim had already gone to the kitchen and made some tea for both of them, their only breakfast.

Our friends had never been to Segovia, so that morning we made up our minds to go there and, besides the sightseeing, enjoy a nice lunch at 'Cándido', the well-known restaurant located almost under the Roman aqueduct. It was Sunday and, fortunately, I took the precaution of booking a table, for the restaurant was full of customers, foreigners and locals. The dining room was attractively decorated in traditional style. There was a big landscape painted on one of the walls, under the wooden coffered ceiling, and Austin was much interested in the old framed photographs hanging round the room, and the many prizes Cándido had received down the years, which were hung on the walls. As I rightly supposed, both Austin and Yim were delighted with the typical 'Cándido' dish, the suckling pig, which they found delicious. Mercedes and I ordered the no less tasty young lamb, roasted, which I much prefer.

Before lunch we had wandered the streets and looked at some of the many churches dotted about the town. We took, of course, several snaps of the wonderful aqueduct. In the afternoon we went down to the lower part of the town, across the small Eresma river, to have a complete view of the majestic and spectacular castle or fortress called the Alcázar. From our observation post, it seemed we were looking at a giant ship's prow, crowned with its small round towers, protruding over the top of a headland.

Back home, in Madrid, we enjoyed a quiet musical evening.

As a matter of fact, we did not have many quiet moments during the few days Austin and Yim stayed with us. I do not mean to say we were running from place to place, but we did fill our time rather actively. One of Austin's wishes was to visit El Escorial and the Valle de los Caídos, so one day we did this tourist round, which was very successful with our friends. Almost exactly one year later, in one of his letters, he kindly enclosed – as a memento, he said – a copy of his diary's page corresponding to that day. He wrote:

Wednesday 20 May 1992

We made a very gentle start to the day, not going out till 12.30, when Ramón drove us, with Mercedes who was feeling very tired, to El Escorial, which I had wanted to see ever since my Paris student days. Local rainstorm just before we got there, and temperature dropped to about 13 °. Lunched at Chárolas (Charolais), then to the palace, which is less intimidating than I thought, though it certainly reflects the character of its creator, Philip II, even down to the window proportions. 'Impressive rather than beautiful', in Ramón's words. It made me see Mafra in an altogether more favourable light, despite the idiocy of building it. As to the Escorial basilica, Wren must have seen the design before creating St Paul's, and in its time the basilica was definitely the most 'modern' church in Europe. The library has light on both sides, which Mafra hasn't, yet Mafra remains in-comparable. We then drove to the Valle de los Caídos, the basilica formed in the living rock where Franco and the founder of the Falange, José Antonio (Primo de Rivera) are buried. Grand, solemn, dignified, faultlessly simple, truly impressive... but, as Ramón pointed out, 'dedicated to the fallen of one side only'. With my horror of communism, I'm afraid I don't mind; some day it will be seen as a national monument. Back in Madrid, a delightful evening with Ramón at the piano and playing records of songs by Poulenc, Chausson, Roger Quilter. Quiet supper on the terrace (balcony), Mercedes much restored. To bed at midnight.

I would also like to mention the excellent movie we were lucky to see one afternoon. As it was Chinese, produced only the year before, and directed by Zhang Yimou, I thought Austin and Yim might be interested in seeing it, and there we went, the three of us. The film, *Raise the Red Lantern*, starring the beautiful Gong Li, turned out to be a real masterpiece. Gong Li's performance of the tragic 'fourth wife', Songlian, was beyond praise. I realized, with envy, that my companions were able to follow the Chinese dialogue, whereas I had to restrict myself to the English subtitles. I keep an enthusiastic review, written by a certain James Berardinelli a few years later, in which he said *Raise the Red Lantern* was 'one of the more sublimely beautiful and openly disturbing films of the 1990s [...], one of those all-too-rare motion pictures capable of enthralling audience members while they are watching it, then haunting them for hours (or days) thereafter'. I hardly need to say that the three of us were indeed enthralled.

On the last day of their stay we had a dinner party at home, late in the evening because of the heat. As we did three years before, we managed to gather a small group of English-speaking friends, among them Diego and Mimi López Alonso. Diego had been transferred by the bank from Hong Kong to Madrid, where he was then living with his family. Austin, being so fond of and a good historian of Macao, was of course delighted to meet the charming Mimi, herself a Macanese, both finding endless points to talk and discuss about the, then still, Portuguese colony.

In fact, under the circumstances, Macao became the main topic of that evening conversation – the first European outpost on the coast of China. Austin remembered a Macao, now completely lost, 'a fascinating place, charmingly peaceful and quiet' where they could picnic in the middle of the Avenida da Praia Grande without getting in the way of the traffic. That was at the beginning of the 1950s. 'I think,' he said, 'there were twenty-seven cars in the whole town at that time, and nothing ever happened in Macao before eleven in the morning.'

Mimi too was fascinated, hearing of a Macao she never knew. To bring the topic more to the present, Diego recalled a visit we both made to Macao a few years before and the delicious Macanese-Portuguese food we relished at the Pousada de São Tiago. We also paid a visit to the rather romantic Protestant Cemetery, adjacent to the Luís de Camões Museum, to see the tomb of George Chinnery, who was, in my view – at least, to my taste – the greatest painter of the Far East.

To end these souvenirs of Macao and our 'Macanese' party in

Madrid, I can't help copying here the beautiful lines with which Austin closed the Introduction to his book *Macao and the British*:

> Let us therefore approach [Macao] as every foreign traveller in early times had to, being rowed ashore in ship's barge towards the Praia Grande, that elegant crescent of Latin architecture facing the waterfront, beyond which rise the low domes and towers of seminaries and churches, the whole creating that uniquely unexpected European view which is Macao's greeting to every visitor from the sea.

★

Colares, 25 May 1992

My dear Ramón,

This comes to thank you and Mercedes so much for our stay with you, of which we enjoyed every moment. My only fear is lest the two of you were completely exhausted by the time we left. For we certainly fitted in a great deal in a short time, what with the visits to Segovia and El Escorial and the Valle de los Caídos, the excellent Chinese movie, and that delightful dinner party at your home, and our music sessions with those lovely songs of Poulenc, Chausson, and the fascinating one by Bizet, and of course you yourself at the piano (I wish I'd had your piano teacher), so accomplished and seemingly effortless. Really a wonderful visit for us – and I cannot refrain from saying that I think your choice of places at which to eat is impeccable.

I was peculiarly impressed by the Valle de los Caídos, so much so that I spent most of yesterday reading about Franco and his period. There is something very dignified about a man who knows what he had done for his people and lays himself in grandeur and simplicity, commemorating those who died for his cause, and without ostentation, the entire concept hidden in a hill. You rightly drew attention to his tomb bearing solely his name. Impressive in a different way is José Antonio lying there with no surname – on account of his father, I assume, yet there is something extremely sad about it, and of the spirit, which the lack of a surname suggests – and he was the spirit of the Falange. I found the whole place very moving. You will have noted that I said very little as we drove back to Madrid.

Also, thinking it over here, I cannot avoid the conclusion that Franco was right in his judgment of Don Juan. He would have been impossible as a monarch. The one friend I have who, in the Estoril days, knew and greatly admired Don Juan, is himself so 'royalty right or wrong' as to be disconcerting; he is a Papal Duke (claimed to be the oldest dukedom in Europe) married to a Spanish Infanta who is exceedingly beautiful, even now she's an old duck. The husband's quiet references to Don Juan in the 1960s were to me a warning rather than a commendation. I felt instantly that Franco had made the right decision.

El Escorial was a revelation. Since my student days in Paris at the time of the Spanish Civil War (last stages, and on the eve of World War II), one of my hopes had been to go to the Escorial. It never proved possible till this time, with you and Mercedes. I bless you both, and especially Mercedes, who was feeling rather under the weather, none of us having gone to bed till long after 2 a.m. the previous evening. But Mafra was in my mind, that extraordinary palace-cum-basilica-cum-convento near here, built by the King Dom João V, the richest man in Europe and among the six richest in the world. Rather inflated, he wished Portugal – and himself – to have an Escorial. The place gave me the creeps from the first moment I went into it, in 1974. It always gives me the creeps, every time I take visitors round. But after visiting the Escorial, I see Dom João V more clearly. He was a man of great taste, and great income, and Mafra, in terms of comparison between two somewhat daunting buildings, is more elegant – as you mentioned.

But of course the folly of building Mafra when the king didn't need an extra palace anyway... and when mentioning the number of men employed to build it, I understated; in the last year of the works, in order to have the place ready for the king's birthday in 1730 the number of employed was 52,000, and the birthday being in October, the harvest wasn't gathered in.

About the Rizal biography, I am very sold on the idea – your idea – of a Spanish edition for 1996, but I think you will find it too much of a burden to take on the translation yourself. It may be, however, that in the years ahead you will hear of a publisher who might be interested, and there are publishers who have their own 'tame' translators – good ones, too – which might solve the problem; and I can almost certainly obtain finance to pay for such a translation. With Rizal, things have a way of sorting themselves out unexpectedly well, seemingly by chance. In any case, I will in the next weeks prepare the Spanish texts which a translator must have, just on the chance of our having a bit of luck, and I will later this year have a word with Oxford University Press, because they may know of a Spanish publisher who might be interested.

One strange thing about Rizal is that when anything of significance happens concerning him, the weather is always fine. The most surprising instance I had of this was when, about to begin the biography in 1964, I decided to go to Wilhelmsfeld, near Heidelberg. It had been raining in Western Europe for three months; I reached Heidelberg in rain. I lunched with the Director of the *Augenklinik* and the Vicar of Wilhelmsfeld, both of them *rizalistas*. At 2.15, as we were about to rise from the table, the sun came out. 'There you are,' said the Vicar, 'Rizal weather.' We drove to Wilhelmsfeld in glorious sunshine, spent a splendid afternoon there, and at 6.30, when I got back to my hotel in Heidelberg, it was raining again, and it rained, I am told, for another three weeks. The Vicar was quite accustomed to things of this kind; it was he who coined the term 'Rizal weather'.

Again, in Manila, I have known it rain on 29 December, but never on the 30th. It is of record that, ever since the first observance of Rizal Day in 1898, it has never rained on that day. Recently, some indoor photography at the Rizal family house at Calamba was needed urgently in the season of dense cloud; everyone said it was useless to go there; I told them not to fuss; on reaching Calamba the sky cleared beautifully, and stayed clear the whole time we were there; we got the photographs we needed, and returned to Manila in the usual dense cloud. It is extraordinary, but in anything to do with Rizal one is conscious of being helped, even in quite small things like the photographs. The young Filipino Rizalist who drove us with misgivings to Calamba when I told him I thought it would be all right, was paid for his disbelief by his camera breaking down at the crucial moment, the required photographs being taken by Yim – probably just as well.

Yim says he loved his stay with you so much he didn't want to go home. It was indeed, for us, a marvellous visit, and we thank you most dearly.

All love to you both,

Austin

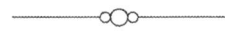

Madrid, 22 June 1992

Dear Austin,

I really don't know how can it be possible that a whole month has gone by since the day you left us – actually we left both of you waving at the railway station. Mercedes told me she talked to you on the telephone and you had had a comfortable trip back to Lisboa, the *Talgo*, for once, not being delayed. And I was very happy when your letter arrived and I could see that you did enjoy your visit to Madrid. Needless to say, it was also such a great pleasure for us to have you both to stay with us for a few days and to visit Segovia and El Escorial with you. I'm very glad you could eventually fulfil your long cherished wish of visiting this impressive monument left by our sad king, Philip II.

After those days of relaxation, my life took again the usual tempo, something between 'allegro vivace' and 'presto' and I came back only yesterday from Düsseldorf where I have been for three days, having several meetings with my Japanese friends.

I believe I can guess what is going through your mind as you read that: 'And this is the one who says he will do the translation of my Rizal?' I must admit it is no easy task, but I would really like to do it or, at least, to have a go. Especially after having finished my second reading. I don't know why, but I have been more deeply impressed now than when I first read the book three years ago (when you very kindly sent it to me from Hong Kong, before we met in Madrid). Maybe this time, with less curiosity to absorb the whole, I went through it more slowly, paying more attention to detail. There is indeed so much in his life – in Rizal himself – that deserves a pause for meditation! I was particularly impressed by his letter to Pastells (4 April 1893) where he so clearly and so convincingly explains his thinking. Perhaps this letter strikes something special within myself, for I feel so much in tune with that thinking. Was not that also, more or less, Unamuno's way of thinking?

And coming to the '*Último Adiós*', I think there is something supernatural in a man capable of writing such a poem when he knows he has but a few hours to live. No less moving is his letter to Paciano and his short messages to Josephine and his parents, which are difficult to read without tears. By the way, have you got the original text in Spanish of all this? I'd very much like to read them, especially the '*Último Adiós*', in Spanish.

As you rightly guessed, there is a copy of Retana's *Vida y Escritos del Dr. José Rizal* in the National Library, in Madrid (in the section called *Hispano-América*, if you please…), although I haven't yet had the time to go there and consult it. But coming back to the translation itself, I'd like to take your own words: 'with Rizal things have a way of sorting themselves out unexpectedly well'. Don't you think that something may happen to help me with my idea? You also wrote in your letter that 'in anything to do with Rizal one is conscious of being helped'.

With the Philippines in mind, I want to congratulate you on the final victory of Fidel Ramos, who was Corazón Aquino's candidate as well as yours.

Unfortunately, the photographs I took in Segovia did not come out as well as I had wished. Nevertheless I'm enclosing some of them which, I hope, can be of your liking. At least they will do as a souvenir of our visit. There is another good one of the aqueduct, which I'm not including, for I remember Yim taking several of it from many angles and I'm sure they will be first class.

The ones I would very much like to have are those taken by Yim at our little party, particularly the last one with the whole group. Will you please remind Yim of that?

After your departure, the weather decided to become very unpleasant and we have had a lot of rain and low temperatures.

Very unusual indeed for June; you came just at the right time, in spring.

I don't know yet whether I am going to make the yearly trip to Japan next autumn, passing through Hong Kong. Anyway, we will be in touch and I will let you know about it.

With my very best regards to Yim and to you,

Yours ever,

Ramón

PS Mercedes sends her love to you both.

Colares, 12 July 1992

Dear Ramón,

Thank you so much for your letter of 22 June, for the photographs – a delightful souvenir of our visit – and for the very nice magazine excerpt with your Japanese associates.

I was so glad you were impressed by that particular letter of Rizal to Pastells, and was interested that you feel the same way as he did; so do I, and I suspect you're right that Unamuno did too, or near enough. Rizal's belief in a spontaneous creation of the universe, with God implied behind it, also strikes a chord with me; and of course his lovely observation that 'revelations' bear the mark of the human fingernail (underlined). We owe his letters to Pastells to Rizal himself; clearly aware of their significance, he made pencil copies of them, and these survived. You enquired about the Spanish originals of these and the death cell letters etc. I can supply the Spanish originals of, I think, everything in the book, and in the next few weeks I propose culling them out and typing them with a view to aiding a Spanish translator of the book. I have also located a copy of Retana; it is in the home of my greatest friend in the Philippines, with whom I usually stay when I go there; he unearthed it recently by accident, not knowing he had it. So this means I can get the Unamuno 'quotes' when I go over to Manila in December.

This means that we have everything in Spanish. As to his letters in German, I have these in facsimile, with a Spanish translation beside them; but the translations are flat and lifeless, giving little idea of the vigour of Rizal's style. My own translations of these letters into English are so accurate that I think they will bear double translation. However, I can send the Spanish translations, if necessary. I will take another look at them; I may have underrated them.

You asked to read the '*Último Adiós*' in the original, and I enclose it herewith, with apologies for the shortcomings of my typewriter, which will not do exclamation marks upside down! I found that typing the poem out was a fascinating experience. My own English translation is, I think, the best in that language; in order to get the meaning across accurately, I deliberately avoided rhyme. But even so I was astonished by the demerits of my translation. The rhythm of the original, its lovely elisions, and the sense of a man talking to his people with an extraordinary authority – all this defies translation. And of course, speaking it aloud – I once spoke a good deal of it to the Spanish Society of Hong Kong – there are absolutely no pitfalls, no awkward breathing problems, no tongue-twisters. I know it is never possible to judge the merits of poetry in another person's language, but to me this poem has a singular grace about it, using simple language as it should be used, and almost designed to be spoken aloud.

As you say, there is something almost supernatural in his writing it when he did; but there is something almost supernatural about Rizal, as Unamuno realized when he read Retana's manuscript. To me, the most unusual thing is how in his novels he describes incidents which later on were to occur in his own life; describing them with such accuracy that in memory one is apt to forget which is the actual incident and which is the fictional. As I put it in a footnote on page 85, I can think of nothing else like this in literature.

Quite clearly, the last poem had been maturing in his mind for some time. '*Mi retiro*', finished just over a year earlier, in Dapitan, to a certain extent foreshadows the '*Último Adiós*'; but of course

'*Mi retiro*' was farewell to his public life, whereas the last poem was farewell to his people, and that is much stronger.

It is also of course a kind of autograph, containing quite a good deal about him, from '*nuestro perdido edén*' – his belief that things were better in pre-Christian-Spanish times – to '*el perdido hogar*' in the last verse – the family home at Calamba destroyed. And I think we have to admit that '*Morir es descansar*' is a statement of faith.

A learned Filipino gentleman, who wrote an entire book on the poem, lamented that in the line about Josephine he had not written '*mi esposa*' instead of '*mi amiga*'. Apart from the latter being better poetry, Rizal was, as usual, telling the truth. The reason he called her his 'wife' in giving her his Thomas à Kempis is that entirely between themselves he regarded her as his wife, and this was a personal gift. Also I think he foresaw that she would return to his native Hong Kong, where she could show the book to others, and the dedication would be a support to her. It was socially the proper thing to do.

Also, the something which was never found, hidden in his shoes, was almost certainly the '*Último Adiós*'. He wrote the poem, then wrote a duplicate; and if I am not mistaken the one which reached the outside world was the duplicate, because it is perfectly written, without a correction anywhere. I tried this one out on Dr Leoncio López-Rizal, who was the greatest of all experts on his uncle's life, and was delighted to find that this had all along been his conclusion too.

Also enclosed are some of Yim's photographs; I particularly like the ones of you at the piano. The colour in some of them is rather peculiar, but we hope you will forgive this. At least, not using a flashbulb, we don't have any of those horrid black shadows on walls. Yim apologizes for the small size of the enlargements. He ordered full-size enlargements, but at Sintra they're not accustomed to such outrageous expenditure, and make them smaller. We are sending duplicates of some of the ones taken at the party, in case you may wish to give them to those concerned. That was a very good evening, wasn't it?

Breaking off for a moment to take another look at my Rizal book, it occurs to me that anyone translating it would be well advised to begin where I began when writing it, on page 5, the birth of Rizal. The Introduction and Conclusion would be much easier to do if done last.

I hope Mercedes likes the photographs. At any rate they're very natural of all of us.

Very dearest regards to you both,

Austin

Monte Carlo, 12 August 1992

Dear Austin,

Very many thanks for your letter of 12 July, for the original of Rizal's '*Último Adiós*' and for Yim's beautiful collection of photographs. Everything arrived when we were about to leave Madrid for our holidays. It actually came when I had gone for a few days in London where, just by chance, I came across a new CD, *Eric Coates conducts Eric Coates*, published by HMV. At first I thought it was a reissue of that album you so kindly gave to me in Colares three years ago, but it wasn't. It is a new compilation where I have discovered, for instance, 'I'll sing for you', such a beautiful orchestral love song. It also includes, besides the two famous 'London Suites', the 'Summer Days Suite' complete, which I hadn't got on CD yet. I think this one is part of a new collection on CD under the name of *Historical Performances*.

On my return from London I tried a couple of times to speak to you on the telephone and tell you the good news but you were not at home. (I'm forgetting to say I wanted to buy another copy for you but at the time there was only one available at the HMV shop. I suppose you won't have any difficulty getting one but if you do, please let me know and I'm sure I'll find another one.)

After having read the Spanish original of the '*Último Adiós*' time after time – always with a sort of shiver – I was really awestruck by such beauty of feelings, ideas, words... I thought there is something almost supernatural in his writing and I would add there is something supernatural too in his patriotism, in his deep and boundless love for his country – '*Mi patria idolatrada, dolor de mis dolores, querida Filipinas...*' – I believe it is difficult to find another instance of such a profound obsession as his with one's country, with one's people, coming from the depths of his heart and slowly leading him to the final sacrifice.

I think you should not underrate your own translation of the poem. In the first place the translation is really beautiful and conveys the full meaning of the poem. You were right to sacrifice rhyme in order to get that meaning in full. Besides, as you rightly put it in your letter, there is something in poetry that defies translation and I would say that the almost musical tones of the '*Último Adiós*' – a 'Pathétique Sonata'? – have to be listened to in Spanish. And, of course, I'm convinced that hearing it spoken aloud, as you spoke it in Hong Kong, must have been a very moving experience.

I entirely agree with you that mentioning Josephine as '*mi amiga*' is much better poetry than '*mi esposa*'. Besides being the truth, it sounds better in Spanish in that particular line, and has to me a greater and more important meaning. After all, a spouse is not always a friend.

I feel very sorry for bothering you with all that typing work you are going to do regarding the Spanish originals. I'm consoling myself thinking that in the end they will aid our intended translation of your book. Thank you so much, all the same. I think that if you eventually go over to Manila in December you'll have more than one opportunity to talk to your friends there of our idea.

As for Yim's photographs there is nothing to forgive. They are really good and we are very happy with those enlargements. So are Mimi and Diego. In fact they are delighted with them, as is Mercedes. The ones with you standing by the piano while I'm playing, make quite a collection of expressions and also make me feel almost an important pianist. I too like them very much.

Please tell Yim I'm reading *Wild Swans* down here, the book by Jung Chang he asked me about in Madrid. It is extremely interesting and deals with a lot of problems very familiar to him.

It also is, in my view, very well written and the narrative is as absorbing as a good novel.

When are you going back to Hong Kong? I'd very much like to see you there in the autumn, although I haven't yet got clear plans.

Very best regards to Yim and all the best to you, as ever,

Very affectionately,

Ramón

PS Lots of love from Mercedes.

I have two good reasons for believing that this letter was never posted. One is that I found the original, or what seemed to be the original, in my file. The second, and more important, is that I never received a reply from Austin and he did not mention it in any of his subsequent writings. I cannot explain, however, even to myself, the reason for this oversight. Again, I cannot be sure. It brings to an end our letters for this year and there is a void for several months on both sides. I was quite busy and travelling a lot, as I told Austin in a short note written after Christmas.

VI: 1993

Madrid, 20 February 1993

Dear Austin,

I've been travelling in the Far East for the last two weeks – Seoul, Peking, Canton and Hong Kong – and tried to telephone your number in Mcdonnell Road from all those places. Unfortunately without reply. I guessed you might be in Manila, Singapore…

I look forward to hearing something from you.

With great affection, as ever,

Ramón

————————○○○————————

Colares, 18 March 1993

Dear Ramón,

Your letter of 20 February, addressed to me in Hong Kong, has just arrived. I am so sorry that you have been trying to telephone me from so many places in Asia – I hope it was a profitable visit. I have meanwhile been trying to contact you at your Madrid number, with equal lack of success – including yesterday evening.

The enclosed card will explain all – or some – on my side. Yim and I went back to Hong Kong in early December with the express purpose of moving the pictures and what remained of both our libraries to Portugal. Then, in Hong Kong, with the imminent prospect of the flat looking awfully bare, it seemed to me that we might just as well move entirely. So, at rather short notice, we did. We actually left on 23 January, Chinese New Year's Day – in pouring rain and an icy wind.

In fact, flying to Hong Kong last December, we both, without saying so at first, had the same curious 'end of the chapter' feeling. In the air, we had been reading the Hong Kong newspapers in silence for some time, when Yim put his newspaper down, and said, 'This is no longer our dynasty.'

The words didn't say much, yet they said everything; and it would be impossible to explain them. When we got to Hong Kong, little things contributed to the feeling of being on the way out. As an example, there was no longer any newspaper delivery in our area; Yim had to go down to the Peak Tram terminus, or even to the Hilton, to buy the morning newspapers; and then, with that frightfully steep ascent to be considered, take a bus back. It reminded me of my first week in Hong Kong in May 1949, when I had no morning paper and did not know how to find an English-language one. Entry and departure having certain things in common, Yim's daily early-morning sortie bore the scent of departure.

Then, there being nothing we could do about packing and shipping over the holiday season, we went off to Manila and Singapore. In any case I had to do a book signing in Manila on 23 December – a reprint of my Rizal biography. We left Hong Kong on the Winter Solstice, flew from Manila to Singapore on Christmas Day, and finally left Hong Kong on Chinese New Year's Day – three festivals sacred to the land from which we took off. But it seemed the most sensible way of doing it.

Singapore was a relief after Hong Kong; no one was running away. Kok Seng met us, and we melted into a familiar atmosphere. Melted? No, by luck it was amazingly cool – overcast throughout our entire stay, with just the correct amount of equatorial rain.

Back in Hong Kong, now firmly decided to leave, we had exactly two and a half weeks in which to do it, before Chinese New Year brought things to a total stop for at least fifteen days, with an aftermath of backlog orders for packing and shipping. Bearing in mind Yim's desire to be here in winter, which we have never experienced and need to know about for house and garden – we're both in some ways completely Oriental – it was a case of revving up and off. We gave away everything to people who came with trucks to collect it, thus passing nice things on to people who will enjoy them.

The latest reprint of my Rizal biography, done under contract from Oxford by Solidaridad in Manila, is much better than the reprint I sent you. When the hardback arrives, I will send you one; they produced the soft-cover first. The head of Solidaridad – Francisco Sionil José – is a friend of mine of more than forty years' standing. He has done a very good job.

Your suggestion of a Spanish translation of the book to come out in 1996 has, I need hardly say, touches a nerve, or, as a learned Portuguese friend of mine puts it, caused me to vibrate. I realize it may never happen, but just in case, I am going to put all the parts translated from Spanish back into the original, so that if one day a publisher and a translator should come along, the material would be ready.

ASV have produced another Eric Coates disc by Malcolm Nabarro and the East of England Orchestra featuring 'Four Centuries' (1942) preceded by *The Seven Dwarfs Ballet* (1930 and never recorded before), and 'The Jester at the Wedding' (1932) recorded in full for the first time, incredible as it may seem. It was mainly because in those days of 12-inch and 10-inch records, none of the six movements fitted either, and with popular music (where the money came from) the recording companies were dead against turn-overs, and 'The Jester' would have been nothing but. I've got a copy for you, and will send it when I know you are back in Madrid.

I do hope all goes well with you in business. I regard the EEC with increasing gloom, and the linked money system with pessimism. And the unreal magnification of things seems to me to be so unnecessary. French oilseeds threaten economic war with the US; if there were no EEC France and the US could have a tariff war on their own without bothering anybody else. The same with fishing. Spain and Portugal conduct a perpetual small war over fishing grounds, and Spain conducts similar wars with France and England. Now it is coming to Brussels, and the outcome will be sweeping rules to the detriment of Spain and Portugal in favour of France and England, who will in any case continue fighting each other; and no one will be able to do anything about Russia. The outcome is liable to be deprivation and disorder at Spanish fishing ports and general deterioration and more violence on the high seas, because no fisherman, certainly in Spain, is going to obey artificial rules. EEC rules are certain to make things worse by politicising the matter. It would be much better (but with EEC in existence this is impossible) to let the small wars go on, patching them up nation-to-nation when they get out of hand, thereby keeping them small.

Remember the cap you gave Yim? It has been worn so much that the peak has frayed, and it is today being confined to garden wear.

A big hug to Mercedes from us both.

Very dear regards as ever,

Austin

Colares, 1 June 1993

Dear Ramón,

I send herewith the new Eric Coates disc, with apologies for being so slow. Ever since we got here at the end of January things seem to have been one endless succession of interruptions, with an unusually large amount of business matters to attend to – book business, music business and so on – and on top of it all I lost your new telephone number, through failing to put it immediately into my address book. May I please have it again? I'm so sorry.

You have been much in my thoughts. Trying to do business at this time must be really awful, with the EEC, the monetary system, the devaluations. I only wish the Europeans would disentangle themselves and go back to be proper nations again, but of course this is now impossible.

Our things arrived from Hong Kong in April – pictures, books and clothes mainly. We have now three record players, twelve transistor radios, eight clocks, six hygrometers, nine thermometers, three barometers, mountains of shirts, enough shoes for a platoon – and one of our birds has just laid eight eggs.

Yim is being the soul of common sense. Everything went neatly into the garage on arrival, and once he and the gardener had straightened out the firewood and the pine cones, so did the car. He's now going ahead gently, getting things into the house in small quantities, having planned where to put it. We shall not be settled before November, I would imagine, but at least it will be without uproar.

For the third time I have started on my Portugal book, a different start each time, and this time, being now on page 21, for the first time I think I've got it right. This is the main reason I didn't write to you sooner. I was worried, and I don't like writing to you when I'm worried – I don't know why, but it is a mark of our closeness to each other in sympathy of mind. Just yesterday I saw I was on the right track, and thus today I write to you.

The book is not going to be a history. It's me talking about history, just as I talk when taking visitors around, with a slant on the English visitor, and with comparisons with England. It's superficial, but I think it will spread understanding. Also, it's written when necessary in the first person and from here, on the edge of the pine woods beyond Colares. This gives it a kind of earthy simplicity, and, more important, gives me the leverage to be entirely selective. I take my visitors to the places I myself find interesting. Anything which I think is dull in Portuguese history just won't appear.

Just over a year ago, all four of us were together. As a memento, I append my diary for one day of that lovely visit. I give it exactly as I wrote it. [See p.92]

Very dear love to you both,

Austin

Madrid, 23 June 1993

Dear Austin,

What a wonderful surprise I had with the arrival of your letter together with the CD of Eric Coates's music! I must say it made me feel both happy and ashamed, for it came before I wrote in reply to your kind letter of last March. But you have already pointed out my only excuse in the second paragraph of your letter: 'trying to do business at this time – you rightly guessed – must be really awful, with the EEC, the monetary system (can we call it a system at all?), the devaluations…'

Without any intention of dramatizing, I can say this is certainly being one of the most difficult years of my business life. Everything seems so complicated and so devoid of any reasonable solution that I think I would need another sort of miraculous Yim – 'that soul of common sense' – to organize everything within my mind. It is really frustrating to read articles written by those so-called economic pundits proposing totally opposed 'solutions' to the very same problem. But this not only happens in the economy, as you very well know. In many fields of knowledge – especially in those most difficult to grasp, like theosophy or theology – there seem to be pundits galore 'explaining' the unexplainable.

The remarkable thing about your letter is its timing. You will see why. Last week, browsing at a bookshop in Madrid, I found a beautiful book, *Ausencias*, actually a collection of superb photographs (almost no text) taken by one of the best Spanish photographers at different palaces and monasteries, El Escorial among them. It immediately made me think of you and that you would be rather pleased with it. So I took it with me and it will be now – within a postal parcel – somewhere on its way to Colares. It will reach you in due course. I sent it, however, without any letter and it was then, when I was about to write to you, that your letter arrived.

And with it, the lovely music of Eric Coates. So I thank you so very much indeed for everything. I'm especially happy with this disc for the whole programme is new music to me and I would say most of it is, in my opinion, very top class EC music. I'd like, though, to point out the 'Minuet', the 'Humoresque' and the 'Caprice' from 'The Jester', as the most outstanding of all. I do love them. Could it be because this music and I were born in the same year? Certainly the East of England Orchestra and Malcolm Nabarro have done a very good job.

I'm so glad you have started your Portugal book again and much more to read that this time you 'have got it right'. I'm sure you have and your idea of putting yourself 'talking about history' seems to me extremely attractive.

I really envy you, being able to write in perfect peace, 'on the edge of the pine woods beyond Colares'. It sounds like the title of a tone poem by Frederick Delius (although I suppose that Eric Coates was too English to be inspired by a Portuguese landscape). We would like so much to pay a visit to Portugal this year, but it is almost impossible for me to make any plans at this stage. We'll be in touch.

Mercedes joins me sending very dear regards to you and Yim.

Yours ever,

Ramón

★

On 13 July, I had to attend a meeting in Lisbon and made a very short trip there. However, I stayed overnight at the Hotel da Lapa where I had arranged to meet Austin and Yim in the evening. They very kindly drove from Colares and we celebrated most joyfully our unexpected soirée together, enjoying some drinks and a superb dinner. (The Hotel de Lapa was under the same management as The Albatroz, in Cascais, and the quality of the food was also excellent.) Back in Madrid, two days later, I wrote to Austin.

Dear Austin,

How nice and most kind of you it was to take the trouble to come and stay overnight in Lisbon so we could spend an evening together. I must say I was very happy you did it and to see you again after such a long time and enjoy that lovely dinner. I thank you very much indeed for everything. Sometimes it seems that life is too short to do so many things that make us happy.

Enclosed you will find a photocopy of the cover of the Eric Coates CD I told you about. As you may see, there is always something new for me, as it is now in this CD with the recording of the 'Four Ways Suite' and 'Lazy Night'. Unfortunately I haven't yet had the time to sit quietly listening to this music. I'll write to you later about it for tomorrow I'll be driving up to Bilbao (where I have a meeting of the Sociedad Filarmónica) and will of course have plenty of time on the road to enjoy the music.

Mercedes asks me to thank Yim very much for the sweets.

Very dear regards as ever,

Ramón

★

We were, however, out of touch for several months, and at the end of November we received a short handwritten note from Austin, before they went to the Far East again. It was posted in Colares on the 29th:

Love to you both. We're off to Hong Kong on 16 December, then to Manila, Singapore etc., then two weeks in England and Scotland, back here around 1 February. Our travel agent in Hong Kong (Chinese) says The Mandarin is too damned expensive, so we're staying at Furama. The Captain's Bar is quite near, thank goodness.

Austin

I wrote back immediately, on 2 December:

Dear Austin,

How very ashamed I felt yesterday when, back home, I found your card! How long a silence and how many letters thought but yet unwritten! When you wrote to me last June, you quite rightly pointed out the awfulness of doing business at this time. Since then, unfortunately, the awfulness has increased as the situation is getting worse day by day. There must be a limit, an end to this sort of economic chaos, yet I feel unable to say where or when we'll reach it.

But please forgive me for writing in such a gloomy mood. It was, I imagine, what unconsciously kept me from writing to you before this. I'm doing it now at top speed so that this letter may reach Colares before your departure.

Your card has suddenly brought back into my mind pictures of those lands I like so much, both Britain and the Far East. I'm not at all surprised by the information of your Chinese travel agent in Hong Kong regarding The Mandarin prices. After the past devaluations I reckon the HK dollar is, in pesetas, 29% more expensive and probably is the same figure in escudos. I'd love to enjoy a dry martini at Captain's Bar, all the same.

Anyway I think the Furama is a very fine hotel and conven-iently located, as you say, a stone's throw away from The Mandarin. I well remember the delicious lunch we had together at the revolving restaurant a few years ago and have no difficulty imagining Yim enjoying that splendid buffet once more.

When we last met in Lisboa I hadn't had enough time to listen to the first volume of *The Music of Eric Coates* I had bought in London some days before. On the other hand, the second volume you kindly sent me to Madrid, contained music entirely new to me to let me properly assess Malcolm Nabarro's conducting. It obviously was fine but I wouldn't make any special mention of it. After listening, however – and I did it several times – to his rendering of 'The Three Elizabeths', 'London Suite' and, especially, 'By the Sleepy Lagoon', I'm completely on his side. Maybe it's a change of fashion but I do like his 'Sleepy Lagoon' much more than many others. Did you notice that it goes for four minutes instead of the three of Charles Mackerras? Definitely much more misty and sleepy. The 'Ballad for Strings', which I now know almost by heart, is a fine and beautiful piece of music, although I'd say somehow apart from his usual style.

Talking of 'The Three Elizabeths', I'm enclosing the notes of a new recording – old, but new to me – conducted by F Fennell. In this I especially like 'Springtime in Angus', but you probably know already this CD. I'm also including some information of a really new recording from Lyrita. Apparently there is another Eric Coates CD coming out soon and conducted by Barry Wordsworth. The sample quality is superb.

Since you are going to Singapore and, no doubt, seeing Tan Kok Seng, I wanted to tell you that I read *Three Sisters of Sz* during the summer and found it most interesting and enjoyable. He has, indisputably, an enormous talent as storyteller.

Both Mercedes and I wish you both a very good trip and the happiest oriental Christmas. Please let me know when you are back in Colares.

Yours ever,

Ramón

My last letter to Austin in 1993 was sent by fax to the Hotel Furama, in Hong Kong, on 17 December:

Dear Austin,

I hope you have had a very comfortable flight. How do you feel arriving in Hong Kong without having a home?

The Argentinian composer I talked to you about is Carlos Guastavino. He has written many beautiful songs and piano music. He used to be a successful concert pianist forty years ago and now, over eighty, lives alone in Buenos Aires. I believe he is a very friendly and charming person, but a shy character.

He told me Marco Polo, in Hong Kong, has published a CD with his complete two-piano and four-hand works, played by Capelli and Moreno, two Argentinian pianists who live in Firenze, and he is quite happy with it. This CD is impossible to find here and it'd be a very great favour if you could get a copy for me there.

The other day I forgot to ask you about the progress of your present writing. How is it going?

I wish both of you all the very best in Manila and Singapore.

Yours ever,

Ramón

VII: 1994–95

After their trip to south-east Asia, Austin and Yim went back to stay at the Furama, in Hong Kong, from where Austin, on 13 January, sent me a handwritten fax:

Dear Ramón,

Klaus Heymann, head of Marco Polo Records, has just been here, and has left a copy of the Guastavino record you asked about.

Yim and I leave for London tomorrow night, and for Lisbon - and home - on Sunday 23rd. At some stage, and at the earliest, we will send the record to you by post.

Forgive the late answer. We have been all over the place - south-east Asia - like flying fish. Last night I went to bed at 10.40 p.m. and woke up at God knows what hour with nearly all my clothes on.

I don't think we are going to do this again.

All love as ever,

Austin

[On the corner of the paper: *Child is out somewhere. No use asking.*]

--------------⚬◯⚬--------------

Madrid, 22 March 1994

My dear Austin,

If I say that nowadays my life is rather hectic it's not merely to excuse my writing late to thank you for the Guastavino recording. Unfortunately it is as true as my need to thank you most sincerely for your kindness. You made me happy indeed. I've had no time yet to write to Mr Guastavino telling him how much I have enjoyed his music, but I was very glad when you said on the telephone you had liked it too.

It's difficult to explain how hard and tough our business is, so it's better not to try to and become a real bore. I'll only say that in all my working life I hardly remember such a trying time. I started February with a trip to Andalucía visiting dealers. Normally I'd have been very pleased to see those places again, mainly Sevilla and Granada, with its unique masterpiece – the Alhambra. Calling on dealers, however, is a completely different story.

A few days afterwards I changed temperature and landscape, and travelled to the new Czech Republic and its old capital, Prague. I was in search of some reasonably priced pianos with a certain quality. Although I'm not sure of having found them and despite the biting cold – minus 8–12 ° – I did enjoy this first visit to Bohemia. I had to go as far as to Jihlava, an attractive small town in Moravia, full of buildings in traditional architectonic style, so I could see some of the countryside as well, under the snow. However, this nation – *Ceska Republika* since last year – has, in my view, a problem of identity; for the name of a country should be independent of its form of government. In the past, under the Habsburgs, it was, as you know, the Kingdom of Bohemia, which included, as it does now, Moravia. Then, why don't they call it simply Bohemia? I was told, however, that Moravia wouldn't tolerate that.

Considering your little sympathy with the communist regimes, I'm inclined to guess you haven't been to Prague, or at least not in the last fifty years. It is indeed a very beautiful city, probably second only to Venice – I'm not talking, of course, of large cities like London, Rome or Paris. I was told the communist authorities left the old buildings in complete decay. Now one can see scaffolding everywhere and a lot of those magnificent houses and palaces already restored to their past splendour, at least from outside. The narrow, Ruritanian-style streets of *Malá Strana* (the Lesser Quarter) would be the perfect setting for *The Prisoner of Zenda*. Above them, on a commanding hill, rises the castle of Hradcany, very famous, as I discovered. Seeing the River Vltava, it is difficult not to hear Smetana's music, and the whole city really is music, art and history. Some people link Prague to Mozart – not unwisely, I would say. I felt, however, that the Bohemian composers' music is the soul of the city. One evening I was driven to Vysehrad, the oldest castle where, it seems, everything started, even the idea of Prague itself. From there I could admire a magnificent view of the city, spread out on both banks of the river.

I was pleasantly surprised by the Black Theatre Prague, a totally original spectacle, quite difficult to explain to you by letter. As the brochure indicated, it is interesting to foreign visitors, not only for being a new form, but also because there are no language barriers. In short, I'm sure you would certainly enjoy tremendously a visit to this romantic old capital.

I spent last week in Frankfurt. Again, gloomy faces everywhere. I couldn't talk to a single person (from any country) who is not suffering from this recession. Which is small consolation. After Easter, in mid-April, I'll probably go to Canton looking for something that can be profitably traded. Even if I'm not successful, I shall at least be pleased to revisit dear old Hong Kong. After all, there are only three years left before a Chinese visa will be required.

I hope both of you are in much better spirits.

With all my best wishes, yours ever,

Ramón

———————◦○◦———————

Madrid, 28 March 1994

Dear Austin,

Yesterday I read this brilliant review – written by your good friend Derek Davies – of Han Suyin's latest book, her biography of Zhou En-lai. (Out of Davies's many equally wise comments, I would like to quote this: 'One would have thought that, after the chorus of contempt which greeted her two-volume hagiography of Mao, *The Morning Deluge* and *Wind in the Tower*, an instinct for self-preservation if not a sense of shame would have inhibited Han Suyin from attempting a biography of Zhou En-lai.') Although I had already ordered it from Hatchards, I must admit I have enjoyed Derek Davies's fine and witty scolding. She always tries the impossible: we say in Spanish, '*Querer nadar y guardar la ropa.*' ('To want to have one's cake and eat it.')

I don't know if you can get *The Financial Times* in Colares and thought you would be glad to read it.

With best regards, yours ever,

Ramón

PS Hope you have already received my letter of a few days ago.

★

During the rest of 1994 and the whole 1995 our letters were very scarce, almost non-existent. For some reason we communicated mostly by telephone. I believe Austin started to feel the first symptoms of the serious illness which, in the end, killed him, but he didn't tell me anything until much later. Probably, without saying so, he didn't feel like writing letters as he usually did. He felt tired. Even so, we talked several times of a possible visit to Madrid in the following year. At the end of December 1995 I wrote from Monte Carlo:

Dear Austin,

As in the title of that old song, 'you go to my head'. As a matter of fact, you have gone to my head very often indeed, in spite of my long silence. More than ever, time has overtaken me and this year

– above all its second half – has been especially hectic. I've travelled to New York, Korea, Japan, Hong Kong and, lately, to London. All within little more than three months, and you know quite well how one feels in this sort of whirlwind.

Thank goodness, business is looking up… but only if one is working hard. On top of my usual work I have to finish in 4–5 months a history of the Sociedad Filarmónica de Bilbao, to be published next year when our Sociedad will be 100 years old. As you can see, I don't have a minute to get bored.

Will you please let me know how things are with you? How is Yim?

Before the years closes, Mercedes and I send our very best wishes to you both for this season and for ever. Shall we see each other in 1996?

Yours ever,

Ramón

VIII: 1996

Colares, 3 January 1996

Dear Ramón,

What a joy to hear from you, and above all to learn that business is doing better! Thank goodness for that. And how you are including the Bilbao Filarmonic centenary into the midst of it I don't know. They are damned lucky to have you to do it, and I don't suppose they realize it.

I imagine Mercedes harps on this point a good deal. Please give her a big hug from us both.

I have thrown away the idea of doing a history of Portugal. The stuff I was producing was trite, and I don't know why. But I do feel I mustn't leave my Oriental field, where I know where I am, which it has to be admitted that in contemporary Europe, I don't. I've one more book to write, and it's germinating – usually between 4 and 6 a.m., between dozes. It will be basically pronged on Hong Kong and Macao, the two ultimate outposts of empire, visible to each other and, when I first knew them, equally useless for any practical purpose.

Et cetera. And it will bring in the route from Lisbon and London, painless history, the British conforming to a Portuguese pattern (they won't like that at all), and generally tidying up a good deal of legend and nonsense before it's too late.

This all began while I was temporarily immobilized. Mid-October I was diagnosed as having cancer of the soft palate, and had two months of radiotherapy, going in daily to Santa María Hospital in Lisbon. Very high standards, I'm thankful to say.

They gave me their verdict last week. Clean bill of health, but I must report for examination once a month. With two visits to the Philippines this year (the Rizal centenary), and a good deal of other travel, this is going to require careful adjustment. But with cancer, you do what you're told, and happily I am looked after by a very understanding and rather sophisticated specialist. All three men responsible for me at the hospital were under forty.

Now, we simply must all of us meet this year. I spend next week in London, and about four weeks in England and Scotland in February–March. I was thinking of an April visit to Madrid, but can adjust to your movements. Let us discuss it nearer the time.

My February visit to London will be to attend the recording sessions (BBC Concert Orchestra) of an Eric Coates CD, taking in short works going back to 1912 which have not been recorded since 1939, and will pretty well bring my father's entire orchestral catalogue on to CD, which is rather good. The conductor is coming to discuss the programme on this coming Sunday in London. Some of the works I cannot remember having heard. It's rather fun.

Yim sends his love to you both – I can't tell you what a help he was during the therapy (feeding me was a nightmare, not least to me) – and we both look forward so much to being together again.

Very affectionately as ever,

Austin

Mandarin Oriental Hotel, Hong Kong, 23 January 1996

Dear Austin,

Thank you so much for your letter, which brought me some mixed feelings: great pleasure hearing from you and also great worries on account of your illness. Thank goodness you say the worst seems to be over and you fortunately are in the hands of very good doctors. I'm happy to see you feel well enough to travel to London and Scotland and are even planning to be in Manila for Rizal's centenary.

Your letter arrived when I was myself about to leave Madrid for a rather long trip, and now I'm close to completing a round-the-world journey, going west – unlike Phileas Fogg. I have been visiting two Kawai plants in North and South Carolina – luckily without snow – and after that I've spent a few days near Los Angeles, in the unattractive town of Anaheim, where the winter NAMM Show takes place every year. As I had something to do in Hong Kong, I decided not to go back to Europe but keep flying west instead. And I'm glad for I had a pleasant flight with Singapore Airlines, which I rate as probably the best airline in the world. (It's a pity it's not so often in my itinerary.) I also did something I haven't done before: crossing the international date line, so one whole day 'disappeared'.

No place seems more appropriate for writing to you than Hong Kong. In a way, I did 'meet' you here for the first time when, just by good luck, I came across *Myself a Mandarin*. Now I believe that your idea of going back to your Oriental field and writing that book about Hong Kong and Macao is simply great. As I told you more than once, I'm convinced you still have several 'Oriental' books hidden somewhere in your mind. After June 1997 nothing will be the same in this part of the world, and your book will be a sort of farewell to the spirit of old Hong Kong, with, as you say, both the British and the Portuguese being mixed up.

I have got some more Eric Coates CDs which I'll show you when you come to Madrid. I too have a heavy travelling schedule for this year, with another trip to the Far East around March–April, but I most definitely agree with you, we must all of us meet this year and your idea of coming to Madrid is splendid.

Depending my work, and if it fits in with your dates, I think it might be around the end of April or the beginning of May, but in any case we'll be in touch and decide later.

With my warmest regards to Yim and looking forward to seeing you very soon,

Yours ever,

Ramón

———————o〇o———————

Madrid, 7 March 1996

Dear Austin,

Looking today for a book about female lied and opera singers, I have come across this one on your friend Rizal. This is, however, a first edition and the texts date back to 1955. Apparently Angel Rodríguez-Bachiller wore the Dominican habit for four years and, most probably, had he read your Rizal he would not have been happy with it. His book seems a pile of rubbish, but all the same I bought this copy for you, thinking you might be interested in having a look at it. They – whoever are they – are of course capitalizing on Rizal's centenary, and that reminds me of your *Rizal*. It must be translated and published in Spanish in 1998, as a celebration of the Philippines' independence hero.

Next week I'll be in Frankfurt, then in Bilbao and will be back around March 20–21. And I look forward very much to seeing you soon.

Yours ever,

Ramón

Madrid, 28 March 1996

Dear Austin,

Thank you very much indeed for your telephone call. Mercedes has told me you were in Granada under the rain… while I was in 'sunny' London, what a pity! As I said, to walk at dusk in fine weather, under the old trees of the Alhambra, listening to the water running down on both sides of your pathway, is almost like walking into some sort of fairy tale.

I've been thinking of your visit to Madrid and concluded that you are quite right. The last week of April will be much better than the first one of May. I've realized that during the long weekend starting 1 May, everything will be rather unpleasant: crowded roads, most restaurants closed, etc., so why don't you come whenever you like during the week starting 22 April? (I'll be back from Valencia on 21 April).

Next week we'll be in Monaco, coming back to Madrid on Sunday, 7 April. I hope that in spite of some rain you will really be enjoying your trip through Andalucía.

I look forward to seeing you in Madrid very soon.

With great affection as ever,

Ramón

★

Austin's trip to Andalucía was, paradoxically, a consequence of his illness. This brought to Colares his close friend and personal assistant for twenty years, Tan Kok Seng, whose books of autobiography have been mentioned several times in these letters. He lived – still lives – in Singapore with his wife, Heung, and the rest of his family, and the sad news of Austin's condition moved him to make a long awaited visit to his old friend in Portugal. These became happy days for Austin, who was delighted with the unexpected visit. This and a better mood prevailing after the painful therapy encouraged him to make that tour with 'the sons' – as he used to call Yim and Seng – through Andalucía.

Back in Portugal, Tan Kok Seng remained in Colares with Austin and Yim, and it was thus, one month later, on the afternoon of 24 April, the three of them arrived in Madrid in Yim's little car. As we had not enough bedrooms in our flat, I had booked lodgings for them – 'Nearby, please,' Austin had asked me – at the Eurobuilding Hotel, just across the street from our place, which they found quite comfortable.

In spite of the long journey, Austin was in good spirits, and the same evening we had dinner together on our small terrace. Mercedes cooked a lovely meal. I was curious to meet Kok Seng for the first time and of course to see how Austin was looking after his treatment. Having read Kok Seng's autobiography, and having heard so much about him from Austin, I would have said I knew him to some extent, but, as it is often the case, the pre-conceived idea did not exactly match the real person. He must have been around sixty, but did not look it, and was much taller than I had imagined, definitely very tall for an Oriental, slim, with an attractive look, jet-black hair and a natural elegance of manner. He didn't talk too much, whether out of shyness or out of politeness I did not know. Anyway, he gave me the impression of having a rather engaging personality.

Austin's appearance also surprised me, but in a different way. His face and body were a bit bloated and he had markedly aged, looking somehow older than he actually was. Fortunately, not a single hint of this surfaced in our lively conversation, which flowed naturally, and we were in our usual high spirits. Austin was visibly happy being together with 'the sons', and we spent a great part of the evening discussing plans for the following days. The temperature on the terrace was quite pleasant, as it should be in mid-spring in Madrid, and Kok Seng, being here for the first time, enjoyed the dry Castilian air, so unlike the humid atmosphere in south-east Asia and his native Singapore. Before leaving for the hotel, he kindly inscribed for me *Son of Singapore* – the first part of his autobiography.

A visit to Toledo was a must for Kok Seng, in Austin's view, so in spite of my many visits to the imperial town, there we went late one morning. The weather, as expected, was fine. The Plaza de Zocodover was as usual bustling with activity, and there we began our stroll, which I kept as short as I could, in view of Austin's limited strength. Once more, we went for lunch to the Hostal del Cardenal. Maybe the restaurant didn't have the best food in town, but the general ambiance and the little garden at the entrance were always a success with foreigners, especially overseas visitors. This garden spreads just between the gate and the main building – both reconstructed in the Moorish style – and was, that morning, bathed in mild sunlight, made milder by the tall cypresses. After lunch we sat there in the shade of an awning. I talked to Austin of the splendid book by Gregorio Marañón, *Toledo y el Greco*, which I was sure would fascinate him, but I didn't know of any English translation. Incidentally, I also explained who Marañon was. (Later on I tried to send Austin a copy of the original Spanish edition of the book, but I found it was long since out of print.)

I had taken with me a little book on Toledo, so I could entertain them by repeating some of the many legends enveloping the actual history of the city and its people, like the one which originated the phrase '*una noche toledana*'. In al-Andalus times, a certain Amrús, trustworthy Governor of the emir Al-Hakam, invited 400 notables of the city to his palace in the Paseo de San Cristobal, and during the dinner party ordered all of them to be executed, in revenge for a rising which cost his son's life. But could any palace in Toledo at that time receive 400 guests? And were the Governor's forces strong enough to liquidate so many people without fighting? 'And we should not forget,' Austin added, 'that in those days every nobleman carried his own sword and dagger.'

In any case, although Kok Seng had the experience of a round-the-world tour, and appeared of course to be genuinely interested in everything we talked about, it seemed to me that all this old Spanish culture was quite far removed from his own mentality; in the same way, for instance, as the culture of the ancient Hermit Kingdom – Korea – might be remote from my understanding.

We decided to pay a visit to Chinchón for the sensible reason that it was within comfortable distance of Madrid, less than one hour's drive eastwards, and it was also a novelty for all of us. After leaving the main highway to Valencia, one has to follow a picturesque narrow road that winds over several low hills before reaching this small town. We drove under the pure blue of the Castilian sky. Chinchón, more a large village than a small town, rightly boasts of having the best preserved square in the whole province, and I knew that Austin would appreciate it. As we confirmed afterwards, it turned out to be the right choice.

The square is fairly large and properly square-shaped. The houses on all sides, no more than two storeys high, are roofed with red tiles, and have beautiful wooden balconies or open galleries that run the length of different façades without a break, some of them resting on stone pillars at the ground floor level. Several houses have been turned into restaurants with good reputations, with some of the tables set out on the balconies most of the year. There are also tables and chairs on the square itself. During the grand public festivities, which take place every year in

August, the square is closed and turned into a bullring, something that is supposed to have happened for the last 500 years.

For lunch, however, we went to the Parador, near the square, where we had already left the car. Here too I tried to balance the quality of food and an attractive *mise en scène*, for the Parador is an interesting stone building, set around a lovely little courtyard. My guidebook said it was an ancient convent of Augustinian friars, restored during the eighteenth century and converted into a hotel in recent years. We took a walk, admiring the cloisters around the yard, and Austin, always passionate for history, looked delighted at every detail. After lunch we went to the square and sat at one of the tables, having coffee and watching the bustling people around. Then, out of a sudden, Yim got up and approached a group of people holding strings of garlic, apparently for sale. He bought a big string and, smiling happily, joined the whole group, allowing me to take an excellent photograph. Not less amusing was the shot I took of him in the centre of the square in the perfect pose of a flamenco dancer. Needless to say, Austin and Kok Seng, watching everything from the table, were laughing out loud, almost in tears. Chinchón is also famous for its *anís*, but none of us were tempted by the strong liqueur.

On our way back to Madrid, Yim and Kok Seng, sitting in the back seats, were absorbed in lively conversation in a Chinese dialect that, I knew, was neither Cantonese, nor Mandarin. I asked Austin, next to me, which one it was. 'Oh yes,' he said, 'now they are talking Chiu Chow.' Obviously, I realized, Austin's knowledge of Chinese dialects was greater than he normally admitted. They told me later that the three of them together could use up to seventeen languages.

As my car was not comfortable for more than four people, these outings were necessarily gentlemen-only affairs. In the evenings we returned to our little terrace, where Mercedes, charming as ever, had drinks and a nice dinner ready for us. They were happy moments in which to remember and recount the different incidents of the day.

Austin had told me how he would like to see Diego López again if he happened to be in Madrid. He was, and before our friends left Madrid we met together for lunch at Gaztelupe, enjoying a very good meal indeed. I was certain this Basque cuisine and the restaurant's specialities were going to please everybody, and so they did. Austin and Diego led the day's conversation which, it goes without saying, embraced the Far East, mainly Hong Kong and Manila, the Philippines and the Filipino people. Commenting on the more than 200,000 Filipinas working in Hong Kong as amahs, or domestic helpers, I repeated one of the Hong Kong jokes among expats: 'If someone on the street smiles at you for no reason, you can be sure she is a Filipina.'

'I agree,' said Austin, nodding. 'That's exactly the Filipino character.'

Several months afterwards Austin still remembered that lunch and part of that conversation, and recalled it in the important speech he delivered in Manila on the occasion of the International Conference on the Centennial of the 1896 Philippine Revolution. It ended thus:

> A few weeks ago in Madrid a young Spanish friend of mine who knows the Philippines said, 'If only we had not killed Rizal, we could have left the Philippines with dignity and goodwill.' The truth. And it was good to hear it from a Spaniard of the younger generation.

On our last evening, Austin wanted to be our host for a good Chinese dinner and asked me to select the place. Not an easy task, I thought, considering that in Hong Kong and Singapore they had the finest possible Chinese restaurants. I decided, after some consideration, that the China Fenix wouldn't be a bad choice. Besides, it was not far from their hotel. It turned out to be, in fact, a fine farewell dinner, Austin having selected the different dishes, including a tasty Peking duck. Talking about food, I asked him which was his favourite Oriental one. 'Oh, it's difficult to say,' he said. 'Well, over many years I have certainly eaten enormous quantities of peculiar food.' After some hesitation, and to my great surprise, he added, smiling, 'But, for instance, my favourite breakfast definitely would be a Korean breakfast, with very hot kimchi and very spicy food, that nearly knocks you out at seven thirty in the morning... I also like south Indian vegetables very much. Brahmin food, is another of my favourites.'

It was amusing to see that Austin, being at heart as British as Kipling, had also like him that Oriental side to his character. During an interview at the BBC in Hong Kong, he admitted that when he was posted to India in the Second World War, he took an immediate liking to the East and this fact completely changed his life. Since then he had become happily integrated into the Oriental world.

Now that I recall those days, I realize that meeting Austin by sheer chance some years ago and discovering our beautiful friendship somehow changed my life too. It has been, at least, an important chapter of it.

I have said it was a farewell dinner, but little did I know – neither of us did – that it really was our farewell. That day, that evening, that dinner would be our last encounter. We never saw each other again. The following day, in the morning, the three of them set off for Salamanca in Yim's little car.

★

Madrid, 15 June 1996

My dear Austin,

Though I'm writing with my usual and inexcusable delay, I'm sure you will be kind enough to excuse the inexcusable. Actually for the last couple of weeks I had in mind writing to you, and luckily your telephone call of yesterday evening gave me the final push. Thank you very much indeed.

I was very glad to learn that you are, thank God, getting better and progressing favourably, albeit rather slowly. I imagine that you may feel in a way like travelling across the Gobi Desert on foot. On the other hand, you should know that each day brings the finishing line nearer.

Herewith you will find some photographs 'my camera took' – Yim and I being alternately just the shooters – in Toledo and Chinchón. I hope they will be for you, as for us they are, visible and happy memories of your last visit to Madrid. I think the two snaps of Yim in Chinchón – one with the strings of garlic and another posing as a flamenco dancer – are very amusing indeed.

Meeting Kok Seng was a delightful surprise for both Mercedes and me. As I told you on the telephone, he impressed us deeply as a charming and loving man. He wrote to us a very nice letter from Singapore. I have managed to reread his three volumes of autobiography, enjoying them much more this time, for I could see him coming out from the printed pages. I believe it was a bright idea to refer to you as Kao Tzé in the East and as Austin in the West. By the way, has Kao Tzé any particular meaning? Who gave you this Chinese name?

[Later on I remembered what he had written in the last pages of *Myself a Mandarin*. When he left the Hong Kong Government Service in 1957, he was more than content to record that the only memorial to him was an inscription on a bridge built with the help of the District Office. The plaque was headed by his Chinese name, *Kao Tzé*, meaning 'High Endeavour', and at no stage revealed that he was a Westerner.]

I'm very glad too you feel like giving that long speech in Manila and have found the strength to do it. I'm sure it will be a grand occasion and a proud day for you. Will you please keep for me a copy of your speech? I shall be much obliged.

You will also find herewith the programme of that centenary concert that prevented us going with you to Salamanca. I believe I should explain, though, something about '*los del Cuartito*'. '*El Cuartito*' – small room, as you know – was the name given to an informal gathering of friends united by their mutual love of music (and to their meeting place). They used to meet there to perform chamber music and to play four-hands piano arrangements of a lot of symphonic music. So there were the roots of what later grew into the Sociedad Filarmónica [de Bilbao].

But talking of music, I must tell you I have got a new CD (Marco Polo) of songs of your father, which is a wonderful discovery. These songs seem to me a bit different from the style I knew and, at the same time, have a familiar tinge. There is also an unusual and very nice piece for viola and piano, 'First Meeting'. But of course you will already be familiar with this CD. Reading the commentary written by Michael Ponder I found out that one of your father's fellow students was a certain York Bowen, whose fine music – and indeed his very existence – I have just discovered through a recent recording. It has been made by an outstanding British pianist, Stephen Hough, whom I consider a genius.

Now I have to say goodbye and go back to struggle with my book on the Sociedad Filarmónica. It reminds me of my student days in one respect: I was always running out of time.

My very best regards to Yim. I wish you as ever all the best.

With great affection,

Ramón

Colares, 27 June 1996

My dear Ramón,

Thank you so much for your delightful letter of the 15th, the Bilbao programme (most interesting, an aspect of Spanish life which outsiders would know little or nothing about), and the splendid photographs.

I'm so glad you've got the Eric Coates Songs disc and that you liked it. Klaus Heymann did it without a word of advance warning. I was struck by the fact that once you get the popular and very successful songs (in their day) out of the way, the songs are so interesting. Several of them I'd never heard before, so I was listening from 'outside', as it were. Quite apart from the melodies, his handling of words is so sensitive. And in the selection of songs, Michael Ponder, who did the record for Heymann, is a man who knows my father's music through and through, a very clever choice.

Isn't Kok Seng a delightful person? I've been so lucky to have him by my side for so long, even today ready to come to the rescue in an emergency. He was simply delighted meeting you and Mercedes, and I'm so glad it was reciprocal. He didn't tell me he was going to write to you; if you're ever in Singapore you'll find it's almost incredible who he knows and what he can get done. It's that lovely air he has. I've always said that if he had a motto it would be 'Bring Happiness'.

As for the photographs, the two 'action' shots of Yim are perfectly lovely. I was amazed at your speed of reaction in photographing him when he made that flamenco posture at Chinchón, and was hoping it would come out well. It's perfect. Also the one with garlic and all those unknown people. And he asks me to say, in conveying his thanks, that the garlic is superb, so fresh today that it could have been in yesterday's market.

The one of me with 'the sons' on either side is so like my father when he wasn't feeling well (and therefore wasn't standing up straight) that it's almost uncanny. It reminded me of the strange moment when, after I got back from Borneo two months after my father's death, my mother and I went to have tea with an elderly lady, a friend of the family, who opened the door to us and nearly fainted, thinking for one frightful moment that I was a ghost.

Yes, I'm going to do this Philippine business; I shall have to. But I must do it in comfort. As your photographs show so correctly, I remain in good health with this cancer affair, but I have markedly aged. So I must do things slowly and in comfort. Before doing that really fearfully long flight from London to Manila, I'm going to have a quiet week in London. I've taken a rented apartment for eight days. This wouldn't be necessary if we were travelling under our own steam. But we are guests of the Philippine Government and have to deal with their Embassy in London. All very hospitable but frightfully inconvenient. [The occasion of this trip was the International Conference on the Centennial of the 1896 Philippine Revolution, held in August at the historic Manila Hotel, where Austin made the important speech which I referred to above. I have a tape recording of his reading, which clearly reveals the great strain he was under.]

In December, when we go again for the centenary of Rizal's death on 30 December, we shall mercifully be paying our own way – giving the orders, as one might say.

On this journey, December–January, which includes Singapore, Hong Kong and Macao in addition to the Rizal Centenary (they are elevating me to a Knight Grand Cross of the Order of

Rizal: how I shall stand up under such a weight of metal I don't know), and an important invitation to stay as guests of the Portuguese Ambassador in Bangkok – he has enlisted me to help in making that marvellous old embassy the central memorial point of Portuguese influence in Asia, rather than Macao, where everything will be either stolen or sold – Yim has suggested that he would like to take me to his birthplace, Vietnam.

This is a nice idea. He says it means just Saigon; anything beyond being a bit dangerous. However, Vietnam being the only country of note in Asia which I have not been to, and with Yim as my host and guide, I think somehow we will be all right.

And it will be in the cool season, which I can stand, even when in Saigon it's not very cool.

Which brings me to yesterday. I had to go into Lisbon for an ear test. Very quick and efficient, and we parked on a pavement 50 metres away. We were in Lisbon for about forty-five minutes all told. And goodness me, were we glad to get back to the cool of Colares! – And to our garden, which at the moment is yielding hundreds and hundreds of apricots, nectarines, and plums.

I hope those damned gamma moths have gone away. I'm sending my Rizal biography reissue under separate cover.

With dear love to you both,

Austin

★

This letter was the last one Austin wrote to me. Things did not go according to his plans. After his official trip to Manila, where he delivered the Revolution's centenary speech I have mentioned, his health took an unfortunate turn for the worse. There was no possibility of any second trip to the Far East, no Rizal's Centenary celebrations, nor the projected visits either to the Portuguese Embassy in Bangkok or Saigon. By that time, at the end of the year, he had had to go into hospital again. Immediately after his return from Manila, at the beginning of September, we could still speak on the telephone, and, although I found him, not surprisingly, rather tired, nevertheless he was glad to have achieved his goal.

At the end of that September, I had to travel to Seoul and Hong Kong, and on my way back stopped for three or four days in Singapore. Kok Seng was waiting for me at the airport, and it was indeed a most delightful visit, Kok Seng being the most charming of hosts. As Austin had said, he was a goldmine of information, and there must have been very few things Singaporean which he didn't know or couldn't talk about. I had been to Singapore ten or eleven years before, and I was surprised by the many changes that had taken place in so relatively short a space of time. One remarkable instance was Chinatown, to the south of the Singapore River. The one I knew consisted of rows of two-storey houses, awfully dilapidated, the old paint peeling off most of them. Actually they were called 'shophouses' for it was common for the Chinese families to live above the shop. It was a painful sight. The new Chinatown had dramatically changed. The streets were clean and manicured. The old houses, keeping their original size, had been nicely revamped or, when necessary, totally rebuilt. Neatly painted in lively colours, they were extremely pleasing to the eye. Even the roof tiles were in two colours. The ones covering the proper roof were red, while the lower ones on the eaves, jutting out like a canopy over the ground floor, were of an appealing bright green. Curiously, Kok Seng told me that one side of his business was to import those green tiles from China and supply them to the builders. (Quite a change from his modest beginnings as an errand boy in the vegetables market of Singapore!)

The venerable Raffles Hotel, much celebrated by international statesmen, Hollywood movie stars, and famous writers like Noël Coward or Somerset Maugham, among others, had also undergone so much necessary renovation and repairs that it looked like a brand new building, barely recognisable. It had lost its old charm somehow, but it certainly seemed much more comfortable now. Kok Seng and I went into the new bar, not to have a Singapore Sling – which I don't like – but some dry martinis. I was amused to see, in spite of the strong air conditioning, electric ceiling fans, no doubt trying to keep a nostalgic link with the past. (The same silly thing had been done at the new Repulse Bay Hotel, in Hong Kong.) The only snacks offered on the tables were bowls full of peanuts in their pods, and Kok Seng felt a bit embarrassed when I pointed out that the wooden floor was carpeted with the empty shells. They made an unpleasant noise when you stepped on them.

On the positive side, I am pleased to remember the Cantonese restaurant (the Shang Palace) at the Shangri-La Hotel where, at lunchtime, one can enjoy a delicious assortment of dim sum, the best in town, in Kok Seng's opinion. As the meal progressed, I definitely agreed with him. I thoroughly relished everything, except the chicken feet, which are delicacies for Chinese people, but I cannot possibly put them into my mouth. His son, Chee, a nice young businessman (named after Austin's Chinese name) joined us in that place, which brings to mind James Hilton and his *Lost Horizon*. Talking of books, Kok Seng explained how Austin had pushed him to write *Son of Singapore* and the rest of his autobiography more than twenty years before. It was an instant success (reprinted many times) and made his name very popular both in Singapore and Hong Kong. We also talked about my translation of Austin's *Rizal*, and I confessed my fear of not finding in Spain any publisher interested in the book after having finished the work. 'Oh,' said Kok Seng, 'I remember many occasions of Austin facing the same difficulty.'

The top-floor restaurant at the Westin Stamford – one of the world's tallest hotels at that time – is another place I would like to remember here. It had the shape of a semicircle and the panoramic view was spectacular. From our table by the window we could see, almost at our feet, the Boat Quay, that beautiful crescent near the mouth of the Singapore River, before it reaches Cavenagh Bridge, its rows of small shophouses being dwarfed by the towering skyscrapers rising behind them. When we were there, the sky was overcast but, according to Kok Seng, on a clear day one could see as far as the Indonesian coast. I must also not forget to say that the food was superb.

Sentosa Island, just 500 metres away from the main island, proved to be a very attractive visit. It has several museums, from the Butterfly Park (with thousands of live butterflies) to the Coralarium, containing more than 2,000 seashells, living corals and other marine life. But the most interesting one to me was the so-called 'Pioneers of Singapore', which actually is an evocative look into Singapore's history. This is told through different tableaux arranged with life-size wax figures, more than a hundred in total. However the most impressive of all, in my view, were the waxworks of the Surrender Chamber, showing the British surrender to the Japanese during the Second World War and the Japanese surrender to the Allied forces at the end of the war, describing both moments with much realism. I had read years before an extremely well-written book – JG Farrell's *The Singapore Grip* – recounting the whole drama of those war days, and this visit was telling everything once again. A bit embarrassing, I thought, for Japanese visitors.

Eventually one evening, I met the whole of Kok Seng's family. I was asked to dinner at their place, a nice apartment in Clementi Avenue. What a delightful meeting! There they were, Heung, Kok Seng's charming wife, Chee, his daughter Beverly, an enchanting little child, and a pretty Vietnamese girl whose name escapes me now. I almost knew all of them, partly through Kok Seng's books and, above all, through Austin talking about them. One could not avoid noticing how happy and proud Kok Seng felt of his granddaughter, Beverly. Heung, of whom I had read so much in *Man from Malaysia*, appeared to be, as I had thought, a woman of strong character. No wonder she had been also a pillar of strength in her husband's life! That evening, she cooked a delicious and very Chinese dinner that was celebrated by everybody present. After dinner, Kok Seng calculated it was around noon in Colares and decided we could put a telephone call to Austin. It was a great idea. All of us spoke to him and I had the feeling that it made him especially happy to listen to me being in the middle of 'his family'. His voice, however, sadly betrayed his strain and the advance of his illness. Nevertheless, I was happy to hear to him and, all in all, it was a very pleasant evening.

A few weeks afterwards, I wrote my last short letter to Austin.

★

The Connaught, London, 6 November 1996

Dear Austin,

Reading this article made me recall *Myself a Mandarin*. Well, not exactly, but something of that atmosphere. I thought you might be amused with it. [I can't possibly remember what this article was about.]

How are you and how about your health? I should love to hear from you.

I'm glad to be able to tell you that business-wise this year is going much better, thank God, although these days one should say that 'sotto voce', not to be out of tune. I'm now on my way to Los Angeles to attend a professional audio fair. Nothing exciting, of course. My visit to Singapore was short but delightful, as you may guess, and Kok Seng the most charming person on earth. I was very surprised by the changes in old Chinatown, with the rebuilt or revamped shophouses and so many new businesses there. I thought, once more, it's a pity life is too short to do so many things I'd like to do.

I'm still struggling with my book, which I hope to finish – actually I have to – within a month.

Do please let me know about yourself and your recovery. I hope it will be rapid and effective. Give my very best regards to Yim, and all my best wishes to you.

As ever,

Ramón

IX: 1997

Austin's end was a very sad affair. He received my last letter at the hospital, where he had been readmitted in October and eventually spent Christmas. In fact, his journey to the Far East in August had left him exhausted and he came home to Colares a weakened man. From then on his health deteriorated rapidly and he started losing weight. It was obvious to Yim and to the doctors during the first two months of the year that the cruel illness was progressing very fast, and was unstoppable. It was clearly the end.

On 17 March, early in the morning, our telephone rang and Mercedes took the call. I was in bed with flu. She came in tears into the bedroom. 'It was Yim,' she said. 'Austin has just died.'

Even when it is expected, one is never ready for the final blow. I could not explain or describe the sadness of those moments. Austin has gone, I repeated to myself, my dear friend has disappeared from my life for ever…

Kok Seng had arrived on the 15th from Singapore, just to be with Austin those last hours. It was as if he was waiting to say goodbye to his dear old friend before dying. As Yim told me, Austin smiled when he saw Kok Seng enter the room. It was a sad and happy smile at the same time. Soon afterwards he went into a coma and remained thus the following day, a Sunday. On the 17th, before dawn, he quietly passed away. It was only one month left before his seventy-fifth birthday.

Two days later, I felt well enough to drive with Mercedes to Cascais. We arrived at The Albatroz just as the sun was setting, and Yim and Kok Seng came down from Colares to have dinner with us. Kok Seng appeared stronger, but Yim was inconsolable, a completely broken man. In a matter of a few hours he had become, or so he felt, the loneliest person in the world. Austin's body had already been cremated. It was not a cheerful evening at all.

We stayed a couple of days more in Cascais, and the following morning we went up to Colares. In spite of the glorious weather, the small but luxuriant garden and the house in the Rua das Horas de Paz were silent and seemed enveloped in a gloom. Of course, it was only we who were feeling that way. Yim did not, however, forget to bring out some glasses of chilled Raposeira. After being a bit cheered by that, we drove to the coast, to Praia das Maçás. The temperature was warm enough to enjoy lunch almost in the open air at a pleasant local restaurant – 'Oceano'. During lunch we managed to snatch a timid smile from Yim. I keep a photographic proof of that. Maybe the beauty of the day helped to it.

In the evening, we went with Yim and Kok Seng to the Marinha Club, in Cascais. Yim had booked a table in the club restaurant for us and Austin's close friends, Gilbert and Justina Wells, whom we had already met seven years before. They came down from Azenhas do Mar, together with Lully, Justina's sister, and all of us, in spite of the circumstances, enjoyed a rather agreeable dinner. I was glad to see that Yim gained strength from somewhere and was the perfect host. Justina had also been near Austin during his last days at the hospital, and could give me some details. Both sisters were Macanese, very lively and well travelled in that part of the world, which made general conversation easy and very comfortable.

In the morning we left Yim, and Kok Seng came from Colares to say goodbye. Yim very kindly brought along for me some first editions of Austin's books. They must have been with Austin for many years and bore the marks left by the voracious red ants of Sarawak. The terrace of The Albatroz was very quiet at that early hour, and we sat there looking at the beautiful bay. We had been blessed again with a wonderful sunny day, so luminous and lively that it was unthinkable that a death could be the reason for our being there. It was difficult to take our eyes away from the bright blue sea; still more difficult to stand up and take our leave. But we had to. We also had to go – and went – through the distressing moment of embracing our friends, saying goodbye.

Some time afterwards, Yim took Austin's ashes over to England, to lie beside those of his parents. They are now in twelve acres of gardens, in lovely surroundings. The place is called The

Garden of Rest, in Golders Green Crematorium, North London. There, on one of the walls, is a memorial tablet in gilt letters that reads:

In Memory of
ERIC COATES – Composer, 1886–1957
His Wife
PHYLLIS, 1894–1982
Their Son
AUSTIN COATES – Author, 1922–1997

CPSIA information can be obtained
at www.ICGtesting.com
Printed in the USA
LVHW030104220821
695820LV00011B/1004